CLEVER
MAIDS

Also by Valerie Paradiž

Elijah's Cup

CLEVER MAIDS

The Secret History of
THE GRIMM FAIRY TALES

Valerie Paradiž

BASIC
BOOKS

A Member of the Perseus Books Group
New York

Illustrations by Walter Crane. Originally published in *Household Stories from the Collection of the Brothers Grimm*, Macmillan and Company, New York, 1886.

Hardcover first published in 2004 by Basic Books,
A Member of the Perseus Books Group
Paperback first published in 2005 by Basic Books

Books published by Basic Books are available at special discounts for bulk purchases in the United States by corporations, institutions, and other organizations. For more information, please contact the Special Markets Department at the Perseus Books Group, 11 Cambridge Center, Cambridge, MA 02142, or call (617) 252-5298, (800) 255-1514, or e-mail special.markets@perseusbooks.com.

Cataloging-in-Publication data is available from the Library of Congress
HC: ISBN-13 978-0-7382-0917-3; ISBN 0-7382-0917-1
PBK: ISBN-13 978-0-465-05491-6; ISBN 0-465-05491-9

Text design by Trish Wilkinson
Set in 12-point Centaur by Perseus Books Group

1 2 3 4 5 6 7 8 9 10 /07 06 05

For Herbert, Hilde,
Gabi, Jörg, and Stephan

CONTENTS

PROLOGUE

T HE VERY FIRST STORY IN THE FAMOUS ANTHOLOGY OF
fairy tales collected by the brothers Grimm is "The Frog
Prince."[1] It's about a raspy-throated frog with bad manners who
seeks the favor of a lovely, but reluctant, princess. Most of us
think we know the plot: A handsome prince, who has fallen under an evil spell, is trapped inside the body of a frog. Only the
kiss of a princess can restore him to human form. So the frog
sets about following the princess around the castle, croaking
demands: He wants to eat from her little golden plate, and
drink from her little golden cup. The girl's father, like so many
patriarchs in the Grimms' fairy tales, exerts full authority over
his daughter and orders her to grant the frog's every wish. The

sexual innuendo escalates when the frog hops into the princess's bedroom one night and demands to sleep with her in her "pure little bed." If she refuses, he'll tell the king. But there's always an element of surprise in the Grimm fairy tales, and it seems the princess will not be bullied. She picks the frog up and hurls the slimy creature across the room. Splat. He hits the wall and falls to the floor, whereupon he turns into a handsome prince. *Then* they kiss.

Why are the Grimms' fairy tales so compelling? The shock factor of their raunchy humor, sexual and physical violence, and outrageous gender inequity is spellbinding for modern readers who are accustomed to far more innocuous children's literature. The stories' rich narrative strains—of good and evil, of wealthy and poor, of heroic and helpless—penetrate our collective psyche with their mythic portrayals of our humanity, and our inhumanity. We feel a voice speaking to us through the centuries, and that's just what the fairy tales are: stories that have been transmitted orally, generation to generation, from as far back as antiquity and the Middle Ages.

Tracing the development of these narratives, through the fog of time and translation, might seem an impossible task. But there is a surprising history underlying the Grimm tales that transcends their dark origins. Unlike Mother Goose, the brothers Grimm are not mythical figures. They were Jacob and Wilhelm, flesh and blood men. Born respectively in 1785 and 1786 and raised in the kingdom of Hesse, they became two of Europe's most preeminent philological scholars of the nineteenth century who struggled to make a living from their research in the cities of Marburg, Kassel, Göttingen, and later in Berlin, where they both died. Moreover, certain untruths about the brothers have swirled around the fairy tales for nearly two centuries, not least of which is the assumption that the brothers Grimm wrote the stories themselves. But their famous *Children's and Household Fairy Tales,* published in several editions between the years 1812 and 1857, were not original narratives authored by Jacob and Wilhelm. Much like the popular folk song anthologies that circulated during the Romantic Age, the fairy tales were a group effort that required communal scholarship and the dedicated work of multiple contributors. The brothers Grimm selected, compiled, and edited the stories they gathered from many different collaborators.

Even more untrue than the myth of independent authorship is the long-standing myth of the brothers' travels through the countryside, village to village, transcribing stories told to them by farmers and peasants. Jacob and Wilhelm are themselves responsible, at least in part, for perpetuating that image. Though they never directly claimed to have worked in this fashion, they unwittingly created a romantic conceit about their process by hiding the identities of their most crucial collaborators, without whom the stories never would have made it into print. These contributors were neither commoners nor peasants, just as they were not those little fairy tale elves that sweep into the house late at night to take care of the day's unfinished work. They were, in fact, women, and, what's more, they were educated ladies.

Few readers know that more than half of the 210 fairy tales included in the Grimm anthologies had a woman's hand in them, whether they were recorded from her storytelling or recorded by her as she listened to another storyteller. These were the sisters of the Wild, the Hassenpflug, the von Haxthausen, and the von Droste-Hülshoff families. They served as fairy tale think tanks to whom Jacob and Wilhelm Grimm turned for the majority of the stories. The brothers also discovered solo geniuses, such as the amazing Dorothea Viehmann, whose stories, though not widely known today, are arguably some of the most sophisticated in theme and narrative development. The most famous and beloved fairy tales come from these women, stories that, bearing the Grimm name, have made their way into nearly every country and culture in the world: "Red Riding Hood," "Rumplstiltskin," "Cinderella," "Snow White," and "Briar Rose" (or, as it's more popularly known, "Sleeping Beauty"). Other men contributed to the collection as well, of course, but the method of their involvement was different. Rather than transcribe the stories from storytellers or share ones they remembered from childhood, male contributors—who were often scholars and bookish professors—dug up old manuscripts in libraries and copied out forgotten tales to assist the brothers in tracing a history of the genre. Theirs was a textual, solitary pursuit, but that of the female contributors, we'll learn, breathed with living performance and the vitality of the spoken word.

This book is about the forgotten and unknown women of the Grimms' fairy tales, the social climate in which they collected their stories, and the extraordinary collaboration that bridged the gender divisions inherent in romantic culture to bring the stories into print. The years 1807–1815, known as the golden age of collection, are the most vibrant and exciting period in the history of how the Grimm tales came into being. During these critical years, which dramatically coincide with the rise and fall of the regime of Napoleon Bonaparte, female collaborators not only shaped *how* the stories were collected, but they also established, with the brothers, the core Grimm legacy in volumes one and two of the fairy tales.

Bringing the first two volumes of the *Children's and Household Fairy Tales* into print was a painful process. Ultimately, it legitimized the folk tale—often perceived among educated males as trivial, the province of simple illiterates—as worthy of publishing. Only *after* the golden age of collecting, *after* volumes one and two of the stories achieved acclaim, did male scholars begin to step forward in greater numbers as active participants in the project.

This was, after all, the age of German Romanticism and the Napoleonic Wars. Goethe and Schiller had reached the peak of their literary lives, and men of letters were looking back to the medieval age and antiquity with an eye toward reviving old sagas. With this broader fascination for the oral tradition, Jacob and Wilhelm Grimm believed that through the publication of the fairy tales they were preserving the German past, a past which, given French dominion over most of Europe, they feared would soon be snuffed out. Inspired by the watershed publication of *Des Knaben Wunderhorn* (A Boy's Magic Horn), a collection of folk songs compiled by the German Romantic writers, Clemens Brentano and Achim von Arnim, the brothers saw they could launch a complementary collection of fairy tales by using their sister Lotte's friends as sources. Thus, they set out to unearth every folk story ever told in the German tongue, turning first to the daughters of the Wild family, who lived right across the street. These friends of Lotte Grimm were thus the first to contribute to what has become a modern classic, selling second only to the Bible in Western cultures.

When volume one of the *Children's and Household Fairy Tales* was published in 1812, Jacob and Wilhelm didn't credit their female sources by name. Instead, they celebrated, in the foreword to the anthology, the nameless, poetic soul of German culture and its legions of "simple folk" who had passed the tales down through the ages. "Because this poesy is so intimately linked to the first and simplest life," they wrote, "we see in it the foundation for its popular dissemination, for there is no *Volk* [common people] who can do without it. Even the negroes in western Africa delight their children with stories."[2]

Rather than cite their female friends in volume one of the tales by name, the brothers paid homage to their male literary predecessors who, much like them, had brought storytelling into print while laying claim to an art that was in actuality practiced mainly by women. In 1550, Giovan Francesco Straparola had reported stories "told by a circle of ladies" he knew in *Le piacevoli notti* (The Pleasant Nights).[3] Giambattista Basile, in *Lo cunto de li cunti* (The Tale of Tales), published in the mid-1600s, acknowledged his sources as "a group of wizened and misshapen old crones."[4] Finally, in 1697, Charles Perrault, collector of *Contes de ma Mère l'Oye* (Mother Goose Tales), which included such classics as "Bluebeard," "Tom Thumb," and "Puss in Boots," gave credit to grandmothers, old women, and governesses "as his true predecessors."[5]

Lotte Grimm swapped stories with her girlfriends when they met for tea or did their needlework together, a pastime that was popular among young middle-class women of the age who could read and write. Once Jacob and Wilhelm had exhausted this convenient source, they established connections with educated women of the aristocracy, who had the leisure and time to ply the scholar brothers with scores of tales. Though much about these women was brought to the fore in German scholarship in the past forty years, very little has reached a larger audience outside of academic circles. Those who know about the Wilds and the Hassenpflugs are Grimm specialists and folklorists, writing for one another as they disapprovingly shake their heads at the popular assumption, made again and again, that the brothers collected the tales from peasants as they roamed the countryside. This is a very strange phenomenon for a legacy that so thoroughly saturates our culture.

In this narrative history, I hope to bring the buried scholarly discoveries to light, synthesizing all the fragmented reports on women's participation in this major collaboration of the nineteenth century into a cogent whole. Traveling to small towns and cities where the brothers Grimm and their collaborators lived, I met with historians, museum directors, and fairy tale scholars who generously shared their years of expertise and research. I also spent long hours in libraries and archives in Marburg, Kassel, and Berlin, where I poured over letters, old books, and recent scholarly activity in the field, digging up whatever scraps of event and biography I could find about the women. In this book, I have translated all the German material, including the excerpts from the fairy tales, unless otherwise noted.

I find it telling that Jacob and Wilhelm Grimm each contributed only one fairy tale from childhood memory to what would become the famous *Children's and Household Fairy Tales.* The tragedy of their father's premature death snuffed out their childhood overnight. Somehow, their female collaborators helped the brothers redeem the stolen past. Jacob and Wilhelm's unspoken grief and its repair through literary work are what compels me most about the history of the *Children's and Household Fairy Tales,* which extend beyond the Grimm biography into Romantic culture at large. When I read the Grimm fairy tales, I feel the handmaid's presence. I read between the lines the deep gender ironies and paradoxes that riddle the provenance of stories. I think that all readers *feel* these complexities, but don't comprehend why.

With this book, I hope to shed light on the poignant humanness nested everywhere in the intimate process of collecting the tales. Fixing the stories in print required not only unusual men, but unusual women, too, and in a moment when men's own learnedness was replaced with a feeling of irretrievable cultural loss. After all, it was the brothers and their male literary peers who felt a panicky urgency to preserve the vanishing past. But like the surprising plot twist in "The Frog Prince," a woman often stepped into the collecting process in a most affirming manner. The wounded pride of a German male under the egotistical dominion of the French could be restored by her powers of storytelling and so turn the ugly frog into the noble prince he truly was.

THE WIDOW OF STEINAU

Dorothea Grimm was a desperate soul. She had always been overwrought, but the melancholy quickened the day her husband, Philipp, died of pneumonia. That's when her inexplicable headaches began. She took her medicinal drops, perhaps too often, and sat in long silence on a stone bench in the garden. What would become of her six young children?

Before Philipp's death in 1796, the Grimm family had lived the quintessence of bourgeois harmony in Hanau, the market town where Philipp began his promising career as a legal advocate, only a day's ride by carriage east of Frankfurt. Later, when Philipp was promoted to the esteemed position of town magistrate in the service of Elector Wilhelm I, sovereign of the kingdom of Hesse (in what is today central Germany), the family moved to Steinau, another small rural trade center located in the gentle Kinzig Valley, just northeast of Hanau. Dorothea Grimm gave birth to their children while enjoying the modest yet privileged leisure Philipp's income provided. Several servants tended the household, the livestock, the vegetable garden; and the numerous Grimm offspring.

Jacob, the eldest of the siblings, was born in January 1785. Four more boys followed, almost yearly, like well-trained soldiers issuing from Dorothea's womb: Wilhelm in 1786, Karl in 1787, Ferdinand in 1788, and Ludwig in 1790, just one year after the outbreak of the French Revolution. Finally, in 1793, the only girl, Charlotte, to whom everyone gave the diminutive Lotte, was born. Bringing healthy children into the world was a feat for women living in Europe during the late eighteenth century, and Dorothea Grimm was not spared the sad fate of stillbirths and premature deaths. She grieved the loss of three newborns, and as was customary among pious Protestants, each baby's name was carefully entered into the family Bible. These were the nine Grimm progeny, living and dead. The world-renowned brothers Grimm, the men who would one day publish the famous fairy tale anthologies, were Dorothea's two surviving eldest: Jacob and Wilhelm.

Wilhelm's earliest memories of his mother were enveloped in stillness and boredom. He watched as she spent hours gazing into a mirror, but the scene was nothing like that of the vain queen in "Snow White," who commanded her mirror to tell her that she is the fairest of them all. Dorothea's mirror was anchored to an external wall of the house in Hanau: Standing at a window, she gazed into it so that she could watch the bustling street life reflected from below. She was always a distant figure to her boys when they were young, a seemingly intangible reflection of a living person.

In truth, Jacob far preferred the company of Aunt Schlemmer, his father's widowed sister, to that of his own mother. Every day, he and Wilhelm would walk to her house, where they spent more time than in the Grimm home. Juliane Schlemmer was worldly and learned, a childless widow. Because she was supported by her brother Philipp, she had ample time, or at least more time than Dorothea had, to cultivate her own feminine accomplishments and to teach her young nephews their ABCs. She would sit them down and use a long stickpin to point at the letters of the alphabet arrayed in a colorful primer, all the while repeating the sounds of the letters again and again, poking and poking until the pages were full of holes. "Some letters I learned faster and more readily, like *m*, others with more difficulty, for example the difference between *q* and *p*," Jacob wrote years later when his reputation as a linguist had already spread throughout Europe. "I can remember the whole business [of learning the alphabet] so extremely clearly that it could have happened a few weeks ago, and everything else in between was just a dream."[1]

As the boys progressed, Aunt Schlemmer taught them how to read and write. They practiced aloud, sounding out new words from the Bible. She showed them how to hold the quill properly and steadied their small hands with hers as they composed their first letters. Juliane wore a "blue ribbon on her bonnet and knitted with yellow knitting needles," Jacob later remembered in his autobiographical writings. "Mother's [needles] were white."[2]

Unlike her sister-in-law, Dorothea Grimm had little to do with teaching literacy. She could read her own Bible, and she wrote well enough, but in orthography and style, she was far outstripped by her two young boys not long after their formal schooling began. Dorothea did the more practical things, such as bathing the children in warm water mixed with wine. The smell was sickly sweet, and the water stung whenever it accidentally dripped into Jacob's tender ears. Dorothea would also gently comb and delouse his hair. When pressing his face into her body, Jacob fondly remembered, "It always felt good when a louse popped."[3] To lessen the tedium, Dorothea would exclaim she'd just killed a "mean one." Now all she had to do was find its sergeant, a pronouncement that made Jacob wait all the more patiently. When the chore was finished, she'd count the dead lice. The final tally was a telltale sign of how naughty or good Jacob had been of late.

Just about everyone suffered from lice in late-eighteenth-century Germany, and a diligent mother saw to it that her family's scalps were free of the tiny creatures. Such ordinary chores certainly weren't considered a worthy theme for published literature; however, in most of the Grimms' stories, women's work is present everywhere. Fairy tales, as a rule, were all about common life, at least according to the definition Jacob and Wilhelm gave to the genre. In a fantastic, lesser-known story called "The Devil with Three Golden Hairs,"[4] an old woman delouses the devil himself, stroking his head in her lap. "It wasn't long before he fell asleep, puffing and snoring," the story reads. "Then the old granny took hold of one of his golden hairs, yanked it out, and laid it down beside her."

"Ouch!" the devil screams. "What are you up to?"

"I had a bad dream," she answers, "so I grabbed you by the hair."

The devil angrily demands to know what the dream was all about, and the old woman tricks him by telling him a story that ends with a puzzling question. In reply, the devil unwittingly gives her the answer to a secret riddle that the hero of the story, who happens to be eavesdropping nearby, is seeking. Three times the granny snatches a golden hair out of the devil's scalp. Three times she wrenches him from deep slumber and is given the answer to a riddle. Then, taking the three hairs and the answers to the riddles with him, the hero uses them to win a kingdom, a princess, and bags stuffed with gold, in spite of his rank as a lowly commoner.

The brothers' memories of the Hessian peasantry that had surrounded them as children would one day make their way into the fairy tale anthology we know today as Grimms' Fairy Tales. There were the family servants, for example, such as the washer-woman who scrubbed their clothes in the laundry kitchen attached to the courtyard of the house in Hanau. Jacob wrote that sometimes she would put "a drop of brandy on black bread to eat," and the wet nurse, Gretchen, once took him "secretly to the cellar stairs and gave [him] cheese and bread, which was forbidden." Gretchen also told the boys stories, Jacob remembered with a sentimental yearning for the lost past, but, he added, "She was let go when we moved to Steinau and soon died."[5]

The brothers Grimm spent their happiest and most memorable childhood years in Steinau. When the family arrived there in 1791, Jacob and Wilhelm were six and five years old. Their new home was spacious and comfortable, and the boys lived in a state even more gracious than that of Hanau. They loved playing outdoors. As unwitting romantics they collected precious fragments and artifacts from the enchanting natural world, captured ladybugs and then set them free again, lingered near the water mill, or walked the circumference of the old stone rampart that enclosed their village. Even the old medieval castle and its tremendous moat, which dominated the town square, would etch themselves into the memory of the brothers like a scene from a fairy tale.

There were more "simple folk" in Steinau as well, those intriguing, hard-working characters whose daily lives captured the boys' supreme attention: the housemaid Marie, the coachman Müller, the two nurses who helped with the younger siblings, and the maids who milked the cows and tended the livestock. There was also preceptor Zinckhan, the boys' new teacher, who had replaced Aunt Schlemmer soon after the move to Steinau. Zinckhan was very much disliked. "Pedantic, strict, unmethodical, yet very proper and of limited knowledge," Jacob later complained. [6] Zinckhan came to the house every day to give the boys instruction in Latin, religion, and geography. Dorothea listened in on the lessons, relieved that her sister-in-law now had less influence over her sons' development.

Wanting to be near her brother Philipp, Aunt Schlemmer had followed the family in the move to Steinau, but she and Dorothea did not see eye-to-eye in many domestic arenas. They divided up the chores, but had little to do with one another after that; Aunt Schlemmer watching over the garden and fields, Dorothea taking charge of the kitchen and the preparation of food. Dorothea was much younger than Juliane and didn't understand her sister-in-law's emotional dependence upon Philipp, who had raised and supported his sister after the death of their mother when Juliane was a young girl. Juliane, Dorothea felt, meddled in the family's affairs, and she grumbled too much about Dorothea's cooking.

Philipp Grimm was often away from home. His absences increased when the war with France escalated in the wake of the Revolution and his legal duties to Elector Wilhelm dramatically increased. Jacob and Wilhelm's memories of him were few compared with those of the womenfolk in the house. Philipp had a well-ordered library and he vigilantly read the Bible every morning before powdering his hair, pulling on his long boots, and riding off to conduct business. He was a man of integrity and religion, a true son of the Enlightenment, and a member of the rising class of late-eighteenth-century European men who prided themselves on their education. For Philipp, knowledge and reason were the basis of good character.

At first, the war with France was an abstraction to Jacob and Wilhelm, mere talk among the adults, or a story to be enacted in boyish games. When they played outdoors, they gathered acorns and lined them up into rows of opposing armies.

"The doubles were officers," Jacob recalled, and "the twisted ones with gnarly stems were trumpeters and drummers."[7] By the mid-1790s, however, the real horror suddenly became more palpable. This was when Jacob—he was only eight—heard about the violence of the Parisian mobs and the beheading of Louis XVI and Marie Antoinette. The boy was morally pained, and his young mind could not grasp how human beings could commit such atrocities.

Soon the French were making bold claims upon the territories of the Rhineland, including the Grimms' home. By 1795, towns and villages throughout Hesse, even sleepy Steinau, had become overcrowded with regiments of soldiers marching in from Prussia, Austria, and even faraway Russia. Elector Wilhelm joined these nations against France, holding troops ready for a conflict. As more and more people poured into the region, inflation set in, and food became scarce. For now, the family was safe, because Philipp Grimm's education and allegiance to his sovereign buffered them from the poverty and hunger that had stricken the poor and those without property or livestock.

Then, at Christmas that same year, life for the Grimm family changed overnight when Philipp, overworked as he was, suddenly fell ill with pneumonia. At first, after blood was let with leeches and two large blisters were burnt into his skin, recovery seemed possible. But he rallied only for a few days and, after struggling into the New Year, he died in early January. In shock, Dorothea found herself moving her six children into a house shared with four other families. Their spacious residence, reserved for the magistrate of Steinau, had to be vacated immediately for Philipp's replacement.

Death changes family ties. Jacob and Wilhelm were only eleven and ten years old when they began to see their mother in a new light. Dorothea was a widow now, and the boys ached to be older than they were. They wanted to erase their mother's sadness and ward off her despair over money, food, and the younger siblings. Jacob was amazed by the miraculous truce that had occurred between Dorothea and Juliane. United now in their shared experience of losing their husbands to early deaths, the two women clung to one another and attempted to pull the family through its hard fate. Sadly, their reconciliation was short-lived. Juliane, who was herself sickly, was so bereaved by Philipp's passing that she died before the year was over.

Dorothea Grimm was now truly alone. Under the existing law in Hesse, she had no legal authority over her own offspring, so her father assumed guardianship. But it was only a formality. Hermann Zimmer lived far away in Hanau, and he was extremely old. The guidance he offered his grandsons came to them in letters written in a shaky hand. Far more present was Dorothea's sister, Henriette Zimmer, who began sending the family food, medicine, and clothing. Henriette lived seventy-five miles away in Kassel, the capital of the kingdom of Hesse, where she worked as lady-in-waiting to Electress Wilhelmine Karoline, the wife of Wilhelm I.

Young Jacob began corresponding with his Aunt Henriette. His first letters to her, full of awkward expressions of gratitude and loyalty, betrayed a superhuman effort at blanketing the fragility that possessed his soul. He played the gentleman in his correspondence, offering his aunt his devoted service long before he was ripe for such manly gestures. He also assumed premature responsibility for the family purse and sought advice from Henriette about how to bring his mother's financial affairs into order. He kept his aunt abreast of all purchases and debts, and he reported on his mother's hard labors. Having lost all but one of the servants, Dorothea was forced to slaughter the livestock herself to make the sausages that would feed the children.

Appealing to the electress, Henriette managed to secure a yearly dispensation for Dorothea, but the income was too small to support all six children. Jacob and Wilhelm would have to go away to school. Henriette stepped in again, coming to their assistance by finding two places for the boys at the lyceum in Kassel, even though the death of their father had lowered their rank and, on the books, did not permit their enrollment.

"Dearest sister," Henriette wrote to Dorothea on September 4, 1798, in preparation for her nephews' arrival in the capital, "you saw in my last letter that Frau Vollbrecht wants to take on your 2 sons." Frau Vollbrecht's husband was a cook to Wilhelm I, and the couple had an extra room in their small home for Jacob and Wilhelm to share. "Frau Vollbrecht tells me that she can't do better than 5 *Thaler* for board and room for 1 boy monthly. That makes 10 *Thaler* for both," and "they won't get laundry done for free either."[8] Henriette's letter writing was just as lacking as Dorothea's when it came to grammar and proper orthography, but then, the urgency of survival didn't require a well-sculpted sentence to get the point across. She promised to pay for Jacob and Wilhelm's upkeep in Kassel, the money coming from her own savings.

Leaving Steinau was not easy. The brothers were thirteen and fourteen years old. On the day they left, Wilhelm cried as he sat beside the driver of the rented wagon that took them on the first leg of the long journey. "The most vivid moment for me was when we pulled out of town," he later wrote in his memoirs. "I could see in the distance our apiary garden with its white stone post and its red lattice gate. A thick mist blanketed it, and I thought of all the days I had spent there. But now it seemed so far away, as if a great rift lay between us, and as if I were completely cut off and beginning something entirely new."[9]

In Kassel, Wilhelm did not take to the rigors of the lyceum as quickly as his older brother, and Dorothea was swift to admonish him: "My son," she wrote, only days after their arrival,

I'm here to remind you to be diligent. . . . From now on, you must renounce many pleasures. Even if you have the chance, don't seek out too many friendships with other boys, or you'll distract yourself too much and cause the good people in your house trouble. Yes, Wilhelm, make use of this opportunity that God is giving you. Just think what would happen, if heaven took me or your good aunt from this world. It would all come to an end, and you would have to resort to something else. Consider the kind of privileges you and your brother have over your siblings. We cannot give them what we are giving you. You may not compare yourself to other young people in your years when they enjoy pleasures. They probably still have their parents, but you don't have a father any more, and that means a lot. Jacob can be useful to you in your private studies, in [the subjects] you don't know because you're still far behind him. I do hope that you are living in harmony with your brother? You have

your Sundays free. You can write to me then . . . God keep
you both in health and grant you blessings in your studies.
Read this letter from time to time to remind yourself of
diligence.

Your most loyal mother Grimm[10]

Wilhelm rose to Dorothea's challenge and studied dutifully, sharing the same small desk with Jacob by day and sleeping with him in the same bed at night. Still, more letters of
warning arrived, this time from Grandfather Zimmer, who was
becoming ever more enfeebled. "I cannot repeat to both of you
enough," he wrote, "that you consider the purpose of why
you are in your current situation, that is, to apply all your diligence in and outside of your lessons, so that you may establish
your future well-being. . . . Therefore, avoid seductive society.
Seek out the company of reasonable men, from whom you will
always profit."[11]

Keeping apace with Jacob, whose intellect was pliant and
muscular, had its consequences for the more poetically inclined
Wilhelm. The long hours of sitting, often for ten to twelve
each day, chipped away at his health, and during his final year at
the lyceum in 1802, he suffered an attack of scarlet fever. At
first his illness didn't seem to be acute, but then he began having difficulty breathing. "This was soon accompanied by pains
in my chest," he wrote. The walk to the lyceum was "very mean
when the cold wind that often drives across the Friedrichsplatz
[the large square in front of Elector Wilhelm's palace] blew
against me."[12] After a long semester of convalescence, Wilhelm

had become disabled with a mysterious condition. He might have suffered from panic attacks or an extreme form of asthma. He might have been afflicted with heart disease. Whatever it was, the illness would never leave him. It forced him into periodic bed rest for the rest of his life and severely limited his ability to work or exert himself physically. Walking upstairs or traveling on horseback became nearly impossible.

Meanwhile, Dorothea's health was also failing. The trauma of losing Philipp was a stubborn sadness for her, in spite of letters from Henriette and the boys beseeching her to restrain herself. "It could damage your health," Wilhelm pleaded, "which is so precious to all of us."[13] Dorothea found she could confide in her eldest, Jacob: "I got your letter, after seeing you in a dream the night before. I must tell you about it," she wrote to him on a cold November day in 1798. "I was in Kassel at your aunt's, and their Highnesses [the elector and electress] were there too, and they were especially gracious toward me."[14] In the dream, Dorothea's sister appeared and led her to the top of a stairway. All alone, she descended to the bottom, where she encountered a peculiar man, strangely reminiscent of Rumplstiltskin, the devious riddle-worker of one of the most famous fairy tales the brothers Grimm would ever collect. After greeting Dorothea, the mysterious man bade her to enter a dark little room and gave her a chair to sit on. "I asked him his name," she wrote to Jacob. "He wouldn't answer and handed me a card with French written on it."[15] Dorothea was utterly helpless in her dream. Like the heroine of "Rumplstiltskin,"[16] she had no power over the deceitful man because she didn't know his name, and her lack of education—she couldn't read French—was a dark reminder of her powerlessness as a woman. "On the other side of the card," she continued narrating the dream, "was the prettiest painting. [The man] asked me who had done it. I knew right away it was you. Then [he] told me, 'Get up because you're sitting on a chair that has only three legs.' Another man in the corner laughed. It woke me up, and I found myself in bed."[17]

For Jacob, the symbolism of Dorothea's dream was all too clear. Life for his mother and his four small siblings was as insupportable as sitting on a chair with a missing leg. Men had become untrustworthy for the widow of Steinau. They had abandoned her, withheld vital information, mocked her feminine tribulations. But the dream proved to be something of a premonition: Three days later, another letter arrived in Kassel, and it bore dark news. "Dear Jacob and Wilhelm, You will be shocked to hear of the death of your grandfather." By now, Dorothea was reeling with grief and could no longer censor her despair before her young sons. "Because of his death," she wrote, "my worries have grown even more. It's one blow after another for me. My poor head is wretched."[18] Upon the death of her father, Dorothea fell into a permanent melancholic state that would shape the brothers' memories of their mother forever.

As much as the pastoral paradise of Steinau and its common folk would one day find their way into Jacob and Wilhelm's renowned *Children's and Household Fairy Tales,* so would the tragedy of the widow. A stock character in many of the stories, she is portrayed as selfless and courageous, a woman like Dorothea Grimm or Juliane Schlemmer. Yet in the age of the

Napoleonic Wars, a widowed woman was a soul who lived forever on the brink of total catastrophe. "The Wolf and the Seven Goat Kids,"[19] a fairy tale later included in the Grimm collection, had a particular resonance during these harsh times. Many readers and storytellers of the age equated the evil wolf with Napoleon Bonaparte. The story features a widow goat who must leave her seven children alone at home while she goes out and scavenges for food. Before departing, she warns her kids about the conniving wolf and admonishes them not to open the door until she has returned. The wolf soon appears on the scene and attempts to dupe the children into opening the door by telling them he is their mother. They ask for proof, which he supplies by placing his paw—covered in flour to make it appear white like a goat's—on the windowsill. The seven kids believe the wolf and they open the door. Only one escapes. The cunning wolf eats the rest alive.

Dorothea Grimm and her sister, Henriette Zimmer, could not slit open the wolf's belly to free their lost children, as the heroine of "The Wolf and the Seven Goat Kids" does. In real life, the eldest boys were the family's only hope of redeeming the loss of the father. All Dorothea and Henriette could do was pour their money, their hearts, and their hard labor into educating Jacob and Wilhelm. If they did this, sacrificing all else, then perhaps at least one child might survive the wolf.

2

MEN OF LETTERS

A FTER MOVING TO KASSEL, JACOB AND WILHELM WERE
the picture of German industriousness, completing the
curriculum at the lyceum in half the time of their peers. By
1803, they both had committed themselves to the law, just as
their father had done, and moved on to the University of Marburg to further their studies. That they would follow in Philipp's
footsteps was always the presumption back home. Dorothea
could not imagine her boys following any other calling. In her
mind, they were on a clear track to redeeming the family's stolen
bourgeois status, and their incomes would one day allow her to
leave Steinau and the gloomy memories it possessed. If the lost
idyll of Steinau had been the auspicious location of Jacob and

Wilhelm's awakening romantic consciousness, then Marburg was its intellectual continuation. Situated in the narrow valley of the Lahn River, this town of steep, sloping cobblestone roads, secret stairways, and hidden paths was vested with singular natural and architectural beauty. "Oh, what a magnificent region!" Jacob wrote to a former schoolmate from the lyceum shortly after his arrival in Marburg. The spirit of the place, he said, grew

> more romantic and more beautiful with each step, high mountains, but no open hills, instead they're bejeweled with multifarious greens. Meadows and meadow springs. To my left, up on the mountain, the castle, golden in the evening sun. Before me, a small village so concealed by trees that you wouldn't even see it, did not the rising smoke betray [its presence]. I often walk here, and in my deep musing, I see nothing. My thoughts are not here. But then, I sit down beneath a willow tree, and once again I see nothing, except for the lovely surroundings.[1]

Marburg also possessed a rich, long history that gave a generation of young literati a direct view into the hoary past. The castle, perched at the highest point above the steep town and overlooking a labyrinth of half-timbered homes, was first constructed in the twelfth century by one of Marburg's long line of landgraves, the medieval counts who once ruled the region. "On Sunday," Jacob continued, "I had a look at the . . . Church of St. Elizabeth. A true masterpiece in authentic gothic style . . . how solemn its colorful windows, and how spine-chilling the tombs of the landgraves! Shadowy images of the past murmur around us, reminding us of our transience!"[2] Jacob was celebrating his youthful idealism. The mystery of the ages gave him a place to direct his awakening awe for history.

Romanticism in literature and philosophy was not a specifically German phenomenon, but a middle-class, pan-European reaction against the ideals of the Enlightenment. During the socalled Age of Reason, a profound rift had separated the educated elite and the *Volk*, the underprivileged commoners who, in Enlightenment thinking, were nothing more than an uneducated mob. The early Romantic philosopher of Germany, Johann Gottfried Herder, who died in 1803 just as Jacob and Wilhelm were entering their university years, attempted to repair the problem, giving the term *Volk* a new and positive meaning: The common people and the simple way of life were now celebrated as morally superior and a genuine expression of a nation's cultural identity. Second-generation Romantics, Jacob and Wilhelm among them, latched on to Herder's philosophy and took it to new literary levels. For them, the spirit of the *Volk* was represented by old songs, legends, fairy tales, and myths, the discovery and preservation of which became an essential project of Romanticism after 1800.

Even before Napoleon's unstoppable war machine had overtaken all of Europe—it would extend all the way to Moscow by 1812—it was becoming clear to Romantic thinkers that the struggle for the "Enlightened" ideals of liberty, equality, and fraternity fought for in the French Revolution had failed.

Napoleon had not set out to liberate the countries he was invading, as his propaganda claimed, but rather to subdue them under his dominion. The Industrial Revolution only magnified the social upheaval Europe was experiencing. In England and France, where industrialization had occurred at a faster pace, the middle class had established a strong political and intellectual base; but in the German kingdoms, a sense of nationhood and cultural identity developed more slowly.

Jacob and Wilhelm thus had never known the national unity that France and England enjoyed. Hesse was one small part of a federation of more than three hundred sovereign states that comprised the Holy Roman Empire of German Nations. The myriad borders, rulers, and conflicting legal codes of the federation only strengthened the stubborn vestiges of feudalism that impeded the cultivation of a middle class and a national identity. The Enlightenment and Romanticism both came late to Germany, where politics were always more conservative and where a true revolution never took root. In the early 1800s, the brothers Grimm found their tiny kingdom of Hesse wedged between the warring powers of France (to the south and west), Prussia (to the northeast), and the vast Austrian empire (which extended eastward). While these nations contended for power and land through the Napoleonic Wars, the brothers were just beginning to embrace the notion of a unified German nation in which the citizens might participate in governance.

Ultimately, the Grimms' scholarship of folk pathways and philology became the expression of their deep desire for cultural identity, and it all began in Marburg when the brothers, then students, discovered, a new passion for poetry and literature. Though they had always read widely during their lyceum years, Jacob and Wilhelm now turned an eye to the *history* of German literature in a search for its particular illustration of the *Volk* spirit. This literary awakening also marked their first emotional break from home. Having been raised by women, they found the privileged society with educated men of the university to be especially novel and stimulating. Their first most important encounter among such scholars was Friedrich Carl von Savigny, a progressive aristocrat and historian of the law, who took his talented new students as his protégés and rigorously mentored them into a life of research.

"I cannot easily imagine anything else that would have had as great an influence on me as [Savigny's] lectures," Wilhelm wrote about his university years in Marburg. "I believe it was his free expression and spirit, coupled with a simultaneous poise and quietude, that were so attractive and captivating. He spoke openly and looked only from time to time at a single page. The inspiration that he emitted . . . and the insight into the value of historical observation and a true method of scholarship were benefits that I cannot venerate enough. Indeed, I do not know if I ever would have made [my way] onto a path of respectability [without him]."[3]

If education imbued a man with respectability, then Savigny, founder of the school of legal history, was an outstanding model who gracefully fused the study of cultural traditions with his vision of the origins of the law. The past, Savigny believed, bequeathed the present with precious artifacts showing how human beings had conducted and organized themselves through the ages. A systematic, "scientific" study of ancient and medieval texts that traced and footnoted these old customs back through time was the key to interpreting contemporary legal practices. Savigny strongly opposed the concept of *natural law*, as espoused by the thinkers of the Enlightenment, whereby rules of conduct were seen as inherent in the relations between human beings and discoverable only by *reason*. Countering this belief, Savigny taught that the rights of a people were anchored in their own specific history and could be understood only in organic connection with that history, not in some abstracted intellectual process. His methodology was expansive and interdisciplinary. "The graceful manner with which he occasionally read aloud [to us]," such as from "a passage from *Wilhelm Meister* or a song by Goethe, is still very alive in my mind, as if I had just heard him yesterday," Wilhelm reminisced of his professor's rich lectures.[4]

Although he was only a handful of years older than his prize students, Savigny became something of a father figure to Jacob and Wilhelm. He caused the ties to their mother and their patron aunt to loosen as he led the brothers into the male province of the printed word. While Dorothea was at home in Steinau, butchering the livestock and stuffing sausages, Jacob and Wilhelm were scouring the used bookstores and auctions of Marburg. Lacking funds, they borrowed publications wherever they could, and soon Savigny opened the doors of his personal library to them. "I remember walking in the door," Jacob recalled of his first visit there, and "my eyes saw what they had never seen before. [On] the wall to the right, in the far back [was] Bodmer's collection of *Minnelieder*, which I opened for the first time." Jacob soon found himself drawn into the world of the medieval *Minnesänger*, the German version of the French Troubadours. The language he saw on the page was so pure, so strangely naïve, and yet so inscrutably expressive of the complex soul of another era. He was smitten. "Who could have told me back then that [one day] I would read that same book backwards and forwards, possibly twenty times, and never [again] manage without it?"[5]

Free access to books was a boon because money for such purchases was scarce. Sacrifice still remained the theme of everyday living, so Jacob and Wilhelm took to culling and copying out poems and favorite passages from whatever they borrowed. They were indefatigable collectors and they worked hard for their literature, painstakingly transcribing printed texts with quill and ink. The process inscribed itself into their minds with a burning intensity. The university's foremost scholars noticed the brothers' diligence and heaped predictions upon them about their certain future success. There was no turning back from this love affair with language; yet, in spite of the accolades, they "never succeeded at gaining the least amount of support," as Jacob remembered, even though their widowed mother "had been the wife of a magistrate and had raised five sons for the state."[6] Typical of the aristocratic favoritism still present in Hesse, scholarships went to the students from the upper class. Even their father's esteemed social status before his death was of no help to them. Indeed, the loss of Philipp had diminished the brothers' own standing and limited their opportunities in society. In his complaint, Jacob made no mention of Lotte, the only girl of the six Grimm siblings. Women were of little consequence when it came to education and the power of character it bestowed upon a person.

Despite the obstacles of money and rank, Jacob and Wilhelm, at eighteen and nineteen years of age, became intellectual climbers and managed to cultivate relationships with the most important scholars and writers of Marburg. In 1804, Savigny introduced them to his brother-in-law, Clemens Brentano, a prominent Romantic poet, folklorist, and a significant influence on the initiation of the fairy tale project. Jacob and Wilhelm often encountered Brentano in Savigny's home, at what was becoming a habitual salon for the literati of Marburg. Brentano was known for his gift of dramatic recitation. Striking a pose beside the needlework pastoral that hung on the wall of "the green room," where all the literary discussions took place, he read from his own romances. His language was imbued with vigorous, personal emotion reminiscent of Goethe's *The Sorrows of Young Werther,* a classic of the German *Sturm und Drang* period of the 1770s. This watershed novel anticipated many core psychological aspects of Romanticism and revealed the emotional landscape of the internal self as rich literary territory. It also clearly spelled out for the first time the seismic cultural shift that modern Europe was experiencing. In the chaos of this monumental change, bourgeois man took flight into nature and into his own internal life as a means of escaping society. Goethe's protagonist, Werther, who commits suicide, became a prototype for the suffering individual whose melancholy was an inescapable symptom that afflicted an entire generation.

Thirty years later, Goethe's novel had paved the way for Brentano, a temperamental writer whose own life and mental instability epitomized the melancholic existence of a Werther. In spite of Brentano's unsteady nature, which conflicted dramatically with Jacob and Wilhelm's sober carefulness, the brothers deeply admired and even envied their friend. Brentano's legendary library was rich in unparalleled eclecticism, and, most of all, the brothers felt sincere resonance with his intense love for "ancient poesy," the epics of bygone eras, and oral folk traditions.

By January 1805, Jacob had become more of a colleague to Savigny than a student. While on a research tour in France, the professor wrote a letter to his protégé beseeching him to travel to Paris immediately to assist him. "Dearest Aunt," Jacob wrote to Henriette with the news. "In great haste and with the hope that you will receive this letter before Tuesday, so that by Wednesday I may receive your certain reply, I hasten to tell you that all rests with me as to whether I will follow Herr von Savigny's call to Paris. These are the terms: 8 months stay, 10 *Karolin* for the trip, free room and board there, and a free return home. This is perhaps one of the most important moments of my life. I await your counsel, which my beloved mother will almost certainly approve of."[7]

On the same day, Jacob wrote a second letter to Dorothea, begging for permission to join Savigny. In Steinau, Dorothea was very ill, close to death, when the messenger brought Jacob's letter to the door of her home. The family doctor, who happened to be there, knew from the messenger's demeanor that the contents of the letter were of great urgency, and, after enormous hesitation, he read Jacob's words to his sick patient. "Dear Mother, Perhaps never have I written . . . to you with greater uncertainty than now. Herr von Savigny, namely, has made the very attractive proposal from Paris, where he is now staying, that I go there for half a year to assist him in juridical matters." Jacob attempted to lessen the blow by pointing out how good the trip would be for his French. "Upon my return next fall, I would likely be more easily employed."[8] Dorothea was beside herself with fear: The family's only hope for recovery was proposing to cut off his studies at Marburg, only months before his final exams for the law degree.

Clearly, Jacob was undergoing a change of heart, and Dorothea was at too great a distance to prevent it from happening. After hearing no reply from his aunt or mother for some days, he wrote to Henriette once more: "It is absolutely awful that the situation is so pressing, and that I cannot speak to you and mother verbally about it. I must confess that I am entirely decided to undertake this journey, and it is my hope that you are convinced that only well-considered reason leads me to this decision." He would miss his family, he added, but he knew that his mother would be hit the hardest with the news. Her longing to leave Steinau and "the sad life that she has had to live for so many long years" would, by his own actions, "perhaps be destroyed."[9] It's unclear how or whether the women replied, but by the end of January, Jacob had gone to Paris, leaving Wilhelm to attend all the lectures that he had enrolled for at the university. This only doubled Wilhelm's academic burdens and further compromised his health. It also set a precedent in the brothers' relationship that continued for decades: Wilhelm, ever the sickly one, would always be left behind when his more worldly older brother traveled to distant cities of Europe and, in doing so, made a greater name for himself.

❧

All of Paris was astir in the winter of 1805. Napoleon had just been crowned emperor of France. Allying themselves against him, Prussia, Austria, England, and Russia were embarking on a major war that would rage for the next decade. After the harsh, two-week journey by postal coach to Paris, Jacob arrived in the city as much confused about his own life as about the politics of Europe manifested around him. For those he left behind in Hesse, things were equally unsettling. "It's been 14 days since you left," Wilhelm wrote on February 10, "and I can say, without affectation, that my heart is still bleeding. Externally, I've gotten used to your absence, or nearly so, but internally, I have not. That will take a very long time. I find myself writing pages and pages of letters to aunt [Henriette], hoping to find some sort of comfort in them, for there is no one I can turn to."[10]

Jacob wrote to Wilhelm from Paris, though not with the same yearning that his younger brother expressed. His mind was fixed on the work at hand. "Savigny is, as always, astoundingly erudite," he wrote to Wilhelm. "He promised to allow me to read his papers, among which are his notes on the Marburg lectures, which I'm thrilled about. He has collected and acquired many rare things here. I hope to share more about this with you in the future. Right now, I'm still not completely settled in. My work here has been very light so far. I'm copying out excerpts from glosses. Soon, however, we'll be turning to the manuscripts."[11] He had always been the more strident one when it came to methodological research, and now Jacob could work without the usual interruptions of home. The chance to focus was intoxicating.

Hunched over a desk in the Bibliotheque Imperiale, Jacob spent long days copying passages of text from manuscripts dating back to medieval Rome. As days and weeks went by, the solitary hours in the library began to erase his mind of its habitual, familial burdens. Past lives and forgotten stories, Jacob was learning, could set him free from his own human limitations. He even began to allow himself new liberties and frequented the city's many theaters, though the Parisians' infamous public behavior disagreed with his ascetic German nature. "The audience, especially those in the balcony," he wrote to Wilhelm, "have a lot to say, and before curtain, which is always very punctual, they dominate entirely—an unquiet sea of loud voices, whistling, drumming, yelling etc., so that one can't hear a thing. . . . The frequent applause is tiresome. An actor gets a round every time he enters and exits, even if he hasn't yet uttered a single word. In short, not five minutes go by without applause, and each time someone most certainly shrieks. It's possible that, with time, one could get entirely, or at least partially, used to it. Even if I was capable of the latter, it's still an evil habit."[12]

Far away from Germany for the first time, Jacob, albeit in his own stringent manner, had opened himself to possibilities he had stifled since his father's death. He was coming to the conclusion that, no matter what Dorothea and Henriette wanted and hoped for, he never would finish the law degree at Marburg. He wanted something more. Feeling his new independence, he knew he craved rapport with fine, learned men like Savigny, and a life of books and writing, as well. But the thought of his responsibility to his family was too overwhelming. Returning to Hesse would surely limit him, unless, he wrote to Wilhelm, they became scholar brothers "together, in harmony," just as they had worked and lived so closely at the university and the lyceum, because, "dear Wilhelm," he sentimentally added, "we should never part."[13]

The first thing the brothers had to do was build a library, and Jacob spoke to Wilhelm about the wisdom of purchasing books and of the establishment of a base for their research. But the library was a metaphor for a deeper inclination, and it came through in Jacob's letters like a blood oath. Paris, and even Marburg, had shown him that the provincial Kassel, where Dorothea wanted to reunite the family, could not offer the intellectual debate he needed. But if he and Wilhelm committed their minds *to one another*, the dilemma might be solved. Life without rigorous collaboration, he confessed to his brother, would grieve him unto death. "We will live very much withdrawn and isolated in Kassel," he went on, "for we won't have many friends, and I don't like keeping acquaintances. So let us work in concert and cut off all other associations."[14]

It was not at all uncommon for males of the age to correspond with such a "romantic" sentiment. It expressed a deep philosophical bond that had nothing to do with sexual love, yet Jacob and Wilhelm's relationship was extraordinary. For years, they had lived entirely dependent upon one another, parenting themselves alone through puberty and their teen years. Though there is no direct evidence suggesting they had amorous feelings for one another, some Grimm scholars haven't ruled out the possibility. Jacob, who never married, might have loved men in a more than platonic fashion, but if he did, his Reform Calvinist upbringing likely kept him from acting upon such desires.

By August 1805, Dorothea and the younger children had already settled into what would be the family's new home in Kassel; several rented rooms belonging to a local entrepreneur. Jacob, too, had planned to arrive that summer; but on the journey home from Paris, the French army attacked the Austrians at Strasbourg, forcing him and Savigny to take an alternate road. It was mid-October by the time he made it to Marburg to pick up Wilhelm en route to Kassel. The brothers arrived in the city to find that Dorothea had gone to visit her sister Henriette. The sun had already set. Taking a lantern with them, Jacob and Wilhelm set out to find their mother and surprised her on the dark street, illuminating their manly faces for her to see and kiss. How mature they looked. The fine, youthful lines of their jaws and lips had become more deeply etched with experience.

Indeed, they were like two lost sons in a fairy tale returning home after timeless, mythical separation.

While Jacob and Wilhelm sought employment, the youngest boys, Ludwig and Ferdinand, enrolled at the lyceum, and Karl started a job, though it paid a pittance, in the employ of a banker. By now all of Dorothea's children were in their teens and early twenties, except for Lotte, who had just turned twelve. Taking on paternalistic airs, Jacob expressed concern for his only sister, who had grown, remarkably, into a young lady since he had last seen her. He complained that socializing with other young women in Kassel might cause Lotte to take on their bad habits, which were "basically simple-minded and mean" compared to the uncomplicated, naïve grace of the maids of Steinau.[15]

In spite of her brother's disapproval, Lotte made many new friends. Her first acquaintances were the six young women of the Wild family: Lisette, Gretchen, Hanna, Röse, Dortchen, and Mimi. Their father, Rudolf, owned the apothecary right across the street from the Grimms' home in the Marktgasse. In no time, Lotte became something of an honorary member of the family, preferring the company of her "adopted sisters" to that of her five brothers. Wilhelm also enjoyed friendships with the girls and soon formed a reading circle, attended by the young people of both families, that met every Friday evening. In time, other members of the educated middle class of Kassel joined the group. Jacob attended too, though he was forever reticent. The salon offered him nothing of the scholarly rigor he required. On one evening, while the group was listening to a recitation, he became so bored that he fell asleep in his chair.

In spite of their intellectual isolation in Kassel, the brothers corresponded regularly with Savigny and kept up with all
the literary developments of Europe by reading scholarly jour-
nals such as *Die Zeitung für die elegante Welt* (Journal for the Elegant
World), *Die Zeitung für Einsiedler* (Journal for Hermits), and the
Rheinischer Merkur (The Rhine Mercury). They also initiated
their first publication projects at this time. Jacob compiled and
edited an anthology of *Meistergesang,* old German songs dating
to the Middle Ages and early Renaissance; and Wilhelm rendered skillful translations of lyrics from medieval Danish.

The brothers were not alone in the direction their scholarship was taking. Anthologies of folk songs and folk tales
abounded, and like so many literati of the age, Jacob and Wilhelm had been inspired by the watershed publication of *Des
Knaben Wunderhorn* (The Boy's Magic Horn). Published in 1805,
this collection of folk songs, compiled by Clemens Brentano
and the Prussian novelist Achim von Arnim, had rippled
through the culture to great acclaim. Most of the songs of the
Wunderhorn were taken from old almanacs and books dug up by
scholars who had submitted the forgotten treasures to their editors. Jacob and Wilhelm had themselves contributed several
songs after meeting Brentano in Marburg and learning of the
project. Brentano's vision of the *Wunderhorn* was more aesthetic
in nature than that of his co-editor, Arnim, an aristocrat and
political conservative. In the patriarchal tradition of the Prussian landed gentry, Arnim believed that the earth connected
master and servant in a patriotic bond necessary to battle the
threat of Napoleon and the French. But in spite of the editors'

differing philosophies, the intention of the *Wunderhorn* was wholly and typically romantic: It was to reinvigorate folk culture and poetry as a means of repairing the rift between the educated elite and the lower classes.

At its publication, Brentano and Arnim dedicated *Des Knaben Wunderhorn* to Germany's revered literary father, Goethe, who praised their efforts and proclaimed that a copy of the work "should be present in every home where merry people dwell."[16] Goethe's seal of approval reflected the growing cultural appetite for old folk songs and stories. Even at the weekly reading circle that Jacob found so dull, Lotte and the Wild sisters had begun swapping fairy tales with one another.

❧

Not long after the publication of *Des Knaben Wunderhorn,* Jacob secured his first employment. With the assistance of Aunt Henriette and her connections at the court in Kassel, he was offered the position of secretary to the War Commission under Elector Wilhelm I. The salary was a meager 100 *Thaler,* but so long as everyone scrimped and saved, it was enough to sustain the entire family. Wilhelm, meanwhile, passed his exams for the law degree in the spring of 1806. Though Jacob had never completed his university education, the future was looking bright. The Grimm family, and particularly Dorothea, were beginning to enjoy their fledgling stability, and soon even dared to trust it.

Napoleon's victory at Austerlitz in December 1805, however, loomed darkly in the minds of many Europeans. By now, he was esteemed even by his enemies as a truly great commander who was blessed with innate military genius. French confidence soared. On October 14, 1806, just months after Jacob had assumed his new post at the War Commission, Napoleon's Grand Army crushed the Allies in bloody confrontations at Auerstädt and Jena. The outcome was grim. All territory between the Rhine and Elbe Rivers was ceded to the French, bringing to an end the Holy Roman Empire of German Nations, including the kingdom of Hesse and the sovereignty of Elector Wilhelm I. Within weeks, the Grand Army marched on Kassel and occupied the city.

In the midst of such ominous developments, one bright light entered Jacob and Wilhelm's lives. Their friend Brentano arrived in Kassel. His young wife, the writer Sophie Mereau, had died while giving birth some months earlier, and in a reactive flare of grief, Brentano had rushed into a stormy liaison with a sixteen-year-old girl named Auguste Bußman. Like a rake in a fashionable nineteenth-century novel, he had seduced Auguste and essentially abducted her from her home. Then, hastily, he married her. In no time the relationship turned unhappy and antagonistic, and Brentano's sojourn in Kassel, where he had family, was as much a means of abandoning his girl bride as it was a research visit. The comfort and feeling of familial stability that the Grimms exuded in their home and work routines were a balm for Brentano.

"I have here two very dear, dear intimate friends of old German named Grimm," Brentano wrote to Arnim of his stay in Kassel. Taking self-congratulatory credit for the brothers' passion for "ancient poesy," Brentano boasted to Arnim that it was he who first nurtured the young scholars' interest in forgotten literatures when he met them as young students. Now he had rediscovered them, along with the rich deposit of "venerable poems" they had copied out of old books with "extreme delicacy." Brentano likely envied the brothers' diligence and the pages of folk material that they had so assiduously accumulated since their years in Marburg. He also added in his letter to Arnim how "shocked" he was by Jacob and Wilhelm's modesty concerning their accomplishments; and, with an edge of condescension, he pitied the poverty that had prevented them from purchasing the books they had found the poems in. Seeing a gold mine of folk material at their disposal, Brentano urged Arnim to travel to Kassel immediately: "It is extremely urgent that you . . . come here in order to give [our] eternally delayed second portion of the *Wunderhorn* priority."[17]

Arnim, who was married to one of Brentano's sisters, Bettina, arrived in Kassel in November. Soon Savigny joined them, too. New friendships kindled into an intellectual intimacy that would last for decades, and over the course of the next year, Jacob and Wilhelm made significant contributions to the second and third volumes of *Des Knaben Wunderhorn.* Some of the other Grimm siblings participated as well. Ferdinand, who displayed excellent penmanship and enjoyed an uncanny gift for detail, copied out many of the lyrics; and Ludwig, the youngest boy and a budding artist, illustrated the title page of the third volume.

Amid the flurry of compiling folk songs, Arnim introduced Jacob and Wilhelm to two fairy tales that he had received from the artist Philipp Otto Runge. "The Fisherman and His Wife" and "The Juniper Tree"—which would eventually find their way into the Grimms' famous anthology of tales—were purposefully styled by Runge to read like *Plattdeutsch*, a dialect of the northern reaches of Germany. This ploy naturally appealed to Jacob and Wilhelm, who were fascinated by the evolution of the German language through time. Dialects, in part, represented old forms of German, and they also had a strong narrative expressiveness to them. Just as Savigny felt that a history of the law could be documented by tracing the customs of past generations, the brothers, and particularly Jacob, felt they could chart a history of language and grammar by studying the regional specificities embedded in dialects.

In the midst of this collaboration, Napoleon's notoriously incompetent brother, Jerôme Bonaparte, arrived in Kassel and ascended the throne on August 18, 1807, whereupon he proceeded to alienate the citizens of the former Hesse with a courtly lavishness that typified the corrupt culture of the Bonapartes. The brothers' beloved Hesse was given the new name of Westphalia. Indeed, many things that meant home and tradition began to disappear before their eyes. The court of Wilhelm I, including Aunt Zimmer, had to flee Kassel and live in exile. French was declared the official language, and Napoleon's Code Civil, though propagandized as a progressive legal model that secured citizens new freedoms, was promulgated as a means of privileging landowners and pro-Bonaparte aristocrats. Jacob, disgusted by being reassigned to directing supplies to Napoleon's Grand Army, abandoned his position in the War

Commission. Bewildered by the swiftness of the French occupation of the city and the loss of her exiled sister, the sorrows of widowhood returned to Dorothea and her health declined. Her family, for the second time, was falling into poverty.

The only thing that kept Jacob and Wilhelm going during the difficult years of French occupation was their scholarship. Words, language, and the optimistic concept of the *Volk* provided a means for preserving their manhood and their respectability in the face of such loss. Motivated by the very real threat they felt to their Hessian way of life, and urged on by Bettina and Achim von Arnim and Brentano to press forward with their impressive collections of folk material, Jacob and Wilhelm set their sights on editing an anthology of fairy tales. But this time, they wouldn't be turning to manuscripts and out-of-print books for the treasures they were seeking. Their main sources would be their sister Lotte's friends, the girls next door.

CHILD OF MARY

THE FIRST KNOWN TRANSCRIPTION OF A GRIMM FAIRY tale was penned in Wilhelm's hand, as told to him by Gretchen Wild in 1807. Gretchen, the second eldest of the six Wild sisters, was nineteen years old when she recounted "Child of Mary"[1] to Wilhelm, who was by then twenty-one. She remembered the story from her girlhood, and, though hardly known today, it was a standard among young women of the time and one of the rare religious tales that found its way into the Grimm anthology. Together, Gretchen and Wilhelm had sat in a parlor in the Wild's bustling household. Wilhelm, quill in hand, listened carefully to his source, dipping into the inkwell again and again as she spoke aloud.

"On the edge of a forest," the tale went, "there lived a woodcutter and his wife who had only one child, a girl of three years. But they were so poor, they had run out of their daily bread and didn't know what to feed her." For an audience of young female listeners—who were often told such tales by their mothers, aunts, wet nurses, family housekeepers, and washerwomen—the unhappy lot of the heroine was a common fairy tale theme that bound them together in their own shared experience of sacrifice. One day, while he's chopping wood in the forest, "Child of Mary" continues, the woodcutter encounters "a beautiful, towering woman." On her head is a crown of shining stars. She speaks to him: "I am the Virgin Mary, the mother of the Christ Child. You are poor and in need. Bring me your child. I will take it in, mother, and care for it." As one might guess, the woodcutter gives his daughter over to the Virgin, who takes the girl up to heaven.

The girl leads a good life. She eats shortbread, drinks sweet milk, wears clothes made of gold, and plays with the angels. But once the reader has been shown all the blissful luxuries that heaven can offer, the tale warps into a pedantic lesson on proper behavior for girls of a "certain age." The Virgin Mary calls for her young charge on her fourteenth birthday. "Dear child," she says, "I must make a long journey. Here, take these keys to the thirteen doors of the heavenly kingdom into your protection. You may unlock twelve [of the doors] and view the splendors inside. But the thirteenth, to which this tiny key belongs, is forbidden. Guard yourself against opening it, or you will be miserable."

On that note, the Virgin leaves the girl to her own devices. Naturally, she is curious about the doors. Opening the first twelve, she finds each of the holy apostles seated inside them, hallowed in brilliant light. As she moves on to the thirteenth, her little angel-playmates beg her not to open it. "It would be a sin," they caution her. The girl doesn't argue, but "the curiosity in her heart could not be silenced. Instead, it gnawed and poked . . . and would not leave her in peace." One day, when the little angels are otherwise occupied, the girl decides to unlock the forbidden door, just to take a peek inside. As she turns the key in the lock, the door springs wide open; there she beholds the Holy Trinity, suffused in fiery brilliance. She reaches out to touch the wondrous light, whereupon her finger turns to gold. She is struck with mortal fear and her heart pounds wildly in her breast. She tries to wash the gold away, but it will not disappear.

Soon, the Virgin returns from her journey, calls for the girl, and bids her to return the keys. Looking into the girl's eyes as if they were her very soul, the Virgin must ask, "You didn't open the thirteenth door, now did you?" "No," the girl lies, raising her hand to her hammering heart. The lesson is that no sin can be hidden from divinity, and the Virgin, upon seeing the golden finger, repeats the question. "You didn't open the thirteenth door, now did you?" "No," the heroine replies again.

Gretchen Wild had already passed through the years of puberty that are so ritualized in the story she shared with Wilhelm. Hearing a young woman speak the tale aloud, with all its implicit reference to a girl's sexual awakening, must have made his cheeks flush red. Meanwhile, the youngest daughters of the

Wild family, Dortchen and Mimi, were on the cusp of this transformational period and had surely heard their older sister, their mother, or even the housekeeper old Marie, tell the story.

After the heroine of "Child of Mary" denies her sin a third time, the Virgin punishes her. "You did not obey me, and you have lied as well. You are no longer worthy of heaven." Subsequently, our heroine falls into a deep sleep. When she awakens, she is on Earth again, alone in the middle of an ominous forest. She creeps inside the hollow trunk of a tree and makes it her home. She eats nuts and uses leaves to cover her body for warmth. Her clothes eventually wear out and fall off. She is naked. Her hair grows so long that it reaches her ankles and covers her entire body.

One day, a king who happens to be hunting in the forest discovers the enchanting creature. "Who are you?" he asks. "Why are you sitting here in the wilderness?" She cannot answer him, for the Virgin Mary has made her mute. The king decides to bring the unusual girl to his castle, where he dresses her in beautiful clothes and gives her "everything in superabundance." It doesn't matter to him that she cannot speak, the story tells us, for "she was beautiful and exquisite." In fact, it is her silence—or perhaps more fittingly, the absence of her opinions—that causes the king to "love her with all his heart." Soon, they marry.

When the first child is born, the Virgin Mary immediately swoops down from heaven to the young queen's bedside. "If you want to tell the truth and admit that you unlocked the forbidden door," she says, "I will open your mouth and grant you speech again. But if you persist in your sin and stubbornly deny it, then I will take your newborn with me." Of course, our willful heroine denies her sin, and the Virgin whisks the baby away. *Hartnäckigkeit,* or stubbornness, that nasty vice relegated to the worst ills of women, is a motif in many of the tales, and the heroine of "Child of Mary" is a particularly fierce offender. She gives birth to two more babies and persists in denying her sin to the Virgin. After the second and third newborns mysteriously disappear from the castle, the townsfolk, the king's legal councilors, and the king himself accuse the queen of killing the infants and eating them up.

Unable to defend herself because she cannot speak, the young woman is sentenced to death by burning at the stake. Echoes of seventeenth-century European witch hunts lace the narrative, which, passed down as it had been through generations of storytellers, possessed the very artifacts of bygone laws and customs that had so intrigued Savigny and that now passed remarkably over the lips of Gretchen Wild.

Wood is gathered for the execution. The girl is lashed to a post. The fire is lit, but, as the eager flames scorch her feet, "the hard ice of pride" begins to melt. Her heart, the story teaches us, was moved by repentance, and the girl suddenly wishes to confess her sin. This one thought miraculously causes her voice to return. "Yes, Maria! I did it!" she screams. In an instant the heavens cloud up and rain sheets down, dousing the fire. The girl survives, the sky opens again, and a bright light pours forth. The Virgin descends upon the square, bearing the queen's three abducted children in her arms, and proclaims that she "who repents [her] sin and confesses, will be forgiven."

In "Child of Mary," the double-edged sword of silence that had once made the young woman so lovely in the eyes of the king also serves as the very proof of her crime. According to traditional Christian beliefs—held not only when the brothers Grimm lived but also in preceding centuries—silence and obedience were essential feminine virtues. Such expectations of women not only turned up in the Sunday sermon in church, it seems, but also fairly saturated the culture. Young women, as they heard and told the tale of "Child of Mary" and similar cautionary stories, seamlessly inscribed the rules of feminine sexual conduct into their hearts and minds, as if drilling a lesson that must not be forgotten at any cost. They shared such tales casually with one another while performing tedious household chores together, or when attending social gatherings—literary salons, baptismal parties, or the rare festive ball—events that set the scene for courtship and marriage, a looming reality in their own lives. But a tale such as "Child of Mary," in all its ghastly pedantic of women's sexual conduct, was also a pleasure for the Wild girls to share as they sat together in the evenings with their mother and Lotte Grimm, wrapping chocolates in fine paper that their father Rudolf would sell the following day in his apothecary. The sexual symbolism lurking just beneath the surface of the narrative—the illicit opening of doors, the venturing into forbidden new experiences—was thrilling to utter aloud, almost as if the act of voicing one's deepest fears could ward off true bad fortune. The content of the stories women told reflected real lived experience and the particular ordeals they faced as females: the raising of offspring; their beholdenness (economically and legally) to the institution of marriage; the unremitting, menial, and repetitive chores such as spinning, weaving, or even wrapping chocolates in paper. In a society that privileged males with good educations, fairy tales offered a place where the devaluation of their intellect actually provided women and girls with the somewhat subversive and self-affirming opportunity of communicating their experiences outside the privileged realm of books and publishing.

Moreover, general public condescension of both women and children, which relegated them to the vast and nameless group of simple folk, made sharing stories a unifying activity. Gretchen Wild was telling the tale of women's universal silence when she offered her first stories to Wilhelm in 1807. It was this *voice* that the brothers Grimm, steered by a romantic, intellectual urgency to preserve the vanishing German past, would ultimately fix in print. When it came to the sexes, the fairy tale collection would be fraught with paradoxes. For though the Grimms saw their new project as a scholarly exercise and an intellectual means of battling French dominion, their women used the stories to express the hardships of their servile standing in Europe during a war waged by men against men.

From 1807–1808, more stories poured in from the Wild sisters, these serendipitous sources who conveniently lived right across the street. Perhaps Jacob's rigid opinion of the girls of Kassel was shifting a bit as a result. True to form, he soon took up the lead on the project and began transcribing tales with a zeal far more dedicated than Wilhelm's. The work satisfied an acute need for scholarly productivity and proved to him that he was still part of the intellectual life of Europe, even if it had to be from the lonely outpost of Kassel.

❧

The Wild home was a bustling, many-storied affair, full of hallways, stairways, outbuildings, and *women*.[2] The chief household servant, Marie, directed the housekeeping and helped mind Rudolf Wild's apothecary, called The Golden Sun. A pious soul, Marie also kept a good eye on the girls, overseeing their chores and manners alike. Her habits were old-fashioned. She kept birds beneath her bed, which she claimed was good for cleaning the room of insects; and whenever a storm thundered in the skies, she made the girls kneel down and pray together until it had passed. It was Marie's job to wake the young ladies of the house each morning. "Be quick now," she'd say, prodding them from sleep, "the cows are already out" (to pasture). "Ach, Marie," the girls would reply, sleepily making excuses to linger in their beds, "is the goatherd already out [in the fields], too?" Although we have no record of Marie's having told the brothers Grimm stories for their collection, the servant was a significant influence on the Wild daughters, who grew from girls into marriageable young women under her care and supervision.

Of all the daughters in the Wild family, Dortchen became the favorite of the Grimms. She and Lotte, who were only two years apart in age, were devoted friends. Wilhelm liked playing big brother to her and would entertain Dortchen by sending a baby doll down from a high window by way of a string to where she waited on the street below. Mother Grimm also loved Dortchen. After all, they shared the same name (*Dortchen* being the diminutive of *Dorothea*). Often, mother Grimm would even wish aloud that one day Dortchen might become her "second daughter."

Because the Wild family consisted mainly of girls—there was one brother, named Rudolf—daily life was more homebound that that of the Grimm household, which, by contrast, was predominantly male. Jacob and Wilhelm had long lived in towns far away from their mother's oversight and authority, and their thoughts and interests revolved around ideas and current developments in literature. The Wild sisters, on the other hand, mainly had their family to think of, and so they turned their attention not toward ideas but toward their relationships with work and with one another.

Dortchen and Mimi, aged twelve and eleven, respectively, when they first met the Grimms, shared a candy collection. They stored every treat that was given to them in a fancy box, but one day their sister Röse discovered it, and ate it all up. Röse, who was thirteen, was a reader, or at least she wanted to be. She always sat on the back steps of the house with her nose in a travel book called *Cook's Journeys*. It was the least beloved book the girls owned, but then they were given precious few things to read and had to satisfy their curiosity through repeated readings of old volumes that lay around the house.

Of course, they had their prayer books, too, and on Sundays, they wore white dresses to church. Whenever a sister was confirmed, she was allowed to put on white silk with a pinkish sheen that everyone called *blanc rosé*. Dortchen complained about how boring their religion lessons were. Lotte, on the other hand, enjoyed learning all the prayers and songs in church. She knew them by heart and would use them to console herself whenever she was sad.

The girls' father, Rudolf, rarely went out, and he always took his meals at home. He also hated it when his daughters went into society. As they grew into young women, they disliked having to ask him for permission each time they left the house. Even old Marie would scold them and complain that "too much going means too much coming." Keeping track of so many young women of "a certain age" was certainly stressful for Marie.

Rudolf had the reputation of being a generous shopkeeper in Kassel, often accepting junk and other useless objects from the poor rather than money as payment. He could be a grumpy father and sometimes chastised his six daughters, though he exhibited a certain humor when he threatened to have them all colored blue by the town's fabric dyer. The girls' mother would swiftly intervene before Rudolf's impatience escalated. "We must watch ourselves today," she'd croon. "It looks as though we're in for bad weather." Sometimes the girls got a beating. It happened to Dortchen once, when she picked strawberries from another sister's bed in the garden, then, saying that they were from her own bed, gave them to her mother.

Field work and gardening were everyday chores after school, and stories about working the beds abounded, such as the time their aunt lost her gold ring while digging in the soil, then found it the following spring when it came up on the tip of an asparagus. That very same aunt had lost the very same ring before, when it was swallowed by a hen and ended up in the compost that was laid out on the fields. In colder weather, the sisters tended plants in the greenhouse, which was heated by a small wood stove. Inside this cozy place was a miniature cabinet that contained bottles of oil and vinegar. On special occasions, mother Wild made her daughters a salad to eat in the greenhouse, as if they were attending a tea party. Whenever Dorothea Katarina Wild socialized, she wore around her neck a black velvet band with a large golden medallion attached to it. Inside the medallion was a finely painted portrait of her husband, Rudolf.

Lisette, the eldest sister—she was twenty-four years old when she contributed some of her first stories to the fairy tale collection—could speak French, and when Napoleon occupied Kassel, it was her job to talk to the soldiers whenever they came knocking at the door. Jerôme Bonaparte once held a fabulous ball at the palace, which the girls attended. They came home raving about the splendid buffet, which included a sweet little *Madame* in a white silk dress who sat perched atop a fancy *Bonbonière* (a tray of fancy bonbons). But few Germans in the occupied city were pleased with Jerôme's extravagances, and no one dared drink red wine during the French-Westphalian reign: Rumor had it that Jerôme bathed in it and that his servants then bottled and sold it.

While the brothers Grimm assisted Achim von Arnim and Clemens Brentano in collecting German folk songs for *Des Knaben Wunderhorn*, the girls loved singing the songs to one another, just as they liked to swap stories. At the salt market, they used the coins their father had given them to buy *Six New Songs Printed This Year*, a common title for the cheap flyers of folk songs penned by anonymous authors that were sold by peddlers at the festivals and markets. In fact, Achim von Arnim and Clemens Brentano had used many such flyers as a source material for the songs collected in volume one of the *Wunderhorn*. When the girls came home with their lyrics, they always sang them aloud to Rudolf. Mimi's voice was loveliest, and she was always called upon whenever company came.

Jacob and Wilhelm's visits with the daughters of the Wild home were becoming more frequent. Perhaps their "scientific" research had an unspoken amorous side, too. Rudolf Wild wondered what the young people were up to as they moved back and forth across the street between their respective homes. Those Grimm fellows were too learned for him, and besides, they had a reputation in town for mocking others from their well-educated perches. It's true that Jacob did exhibit a sardonic edge, though Wilhelm suffered less from this bad habit. Nevertheless, in spite of Mr. Wild's objections, the brothers managed to gather a good number of stories from his daughters.

As tales accumulated, Jacob and Wilhelm began to see that they were embarked on something that could be as important as the anthology of folk songs that had put their friends Brentano and Arnim on the literary map of Europe. In May 1808, Jacob sent Savigny several transcriptions of stories as a gift for his young daughter, though, in truth, he also wished to impress his mentor with the fidelity with which he had collected them from his storytelling sources.

Among the tales he sent to Savigny was "The Wedding of Mrs. Fox."[3] It was Jacob's all-time favorite and the only story that he contributed to the collection directly from childhood memory. In his mind it was "one of the dearest" and most "poetic" fairy tales;[4] but Arnim, who was otherwise always supportive of the project, despised the narrative for its lewd sexual references. After its publication in the first volume of the fairy tales, he even demanded that Jacob remove "The Wedding of Mrs. Fox" from future editions. Jacob refused, defending the story as "pure and innocent."[5] Arnim was likely responding to the word *Schwanz*, which appears countless times in the story. Translated literally, it means "tail," but in the vernacular it refers to the male sexual organ and would be translated as "dick" or "cock."

"Once upon a time," the disputed story begins, "there was an old fox who had nine tails and who believed that his wife had been untrue to him. So, he decided to test her loyalty, and he stretched himself out beneath a bench [in the kitchen]. Without moving a single member, he pretended to be dead as a doornail." Mrs. Fox, falling for the ruse and believing him to have passed on, goes up to her room and locks the door. Her maid, Miss Cat, remains at the hearth, cooking.

When news gets around that the old fox is dead, a series of bachelor foxes begin knocking at Mrs. Fox's door, begging Miss Cat to let them in so that they might "liberate" Mrs. Fox. Each time a bachelor arrives, the cat goes upstairs and says to her mistress:

"Mrs. Fox, are you there?"

"Ach, yes, my little cat, yes."

"There's a bachelor here to see you."

"My child, what does he look like? Does he have nine slinking *tails* as beautiful as Mr. Fox's were?"

"Ach, no," the cat answers. "He has only one."

"Then I won't have him."

This routine repeats itself nine times, the number of *Schwänze* possessed by each bachelor increasing by a count, until at last a fox with nine tails arrives. Naturally, Mrs. Fox decides to have him. But "when it was time to celebrate the wedding," the story ends on an abruptly violent note, "old Mr. Fox roused himself from beneath the bench, and he beat the living daylights out of the whole bunch." Then he kicks everyone, including Mrs. Fox, out of the house. The End.

Like the Wild home, which, on the surface appeared to be a harmonious and ideal place to spend one's girlhood, the dark undercurrent of paternalistic authority sometimes raises up through the seemingly harmless family anecdotes, such as when Dortchen was beaten for lying about her strawberry patch. With the suddenness of brutality such as that found in "The Wedding of Mrs. Fox," a girl's world could be turned upside down overnight. The potential for severe punishment always lurked around the corner, and, as the fairy tales repeated over and over again, puberty and marriage in particular were times in a young woman's life when a great deal was at stake: her honor, her prospects for happiness, and her material well-being.

Stories such as "Child of Mary" and "The Wedding of Mrs. Fox" betray even the legal inequities that women faced. This was a time when Napoleon's Code Civil, which was particularly reactionary in its handling of women, was systematically enforced in every kingdom the French Grand Army overtook. Marital offences were dealt with harshly and unequally. A man could demand a divorce by simply making the claim that his wife had committed adultery, no evidence required. A woman, on the other hand, could do so only if she could prove that a concubine had been in the home. Cheating on one's husband meant immediate imprisonment, and a woman could be released only if her husband took her back again. Harsh limits were also placed on women's use of money and their ownership of property. In essence, under this ruthless system, a wife's obedience to her husband was a legal duty. This made "The Wedding of Mrs. Fox," passed down from generations, take on new meaning for women during the Napoleonic era. Indeed, many of the Grimms' fairy tales dole out pedantic lessons in feminine virtue and appropriateness. The means of enforcement are often astonishingly violent. Bad girls lose limbs and fingers in punishment for being stubborn, or they willingly allow their hands to be chopped off in selfless acts of sacrifice. Murderous rapists pursue maidens in the woods. Little men threaten to steal a married woman's children away. Girls' fathers abandon them, pledge them to despicable men in wedlock, or sell them to the devil.

The collaboration that Jacob and Wilhelm had begun with the young ladies of the Wild family was a curious one, for they were collecting stories from women who used the tales ultimately as an expression of their own suffering, as "a place from which to speak about their own speechlessness."[6] Even more significant, these young women of the middle class were hardly part of the simple *Volk* that the Romantics idealized, yet the fairy tales they told betrayed a solidarity with commoners that educated males such as Jacob and Wilhelm could only experience second hand—once removed as they were from the oral tradition they so passionately celebrated.

4

THE DILIGENT HANDMAID

"**D**EAR AUNT, PREPARE YOURSELF FOR THE HARSHEST [news] that you could hear from us," Jacob wrote to Henriette on May 27, 1808. "This morning at quarter of 7 our most beloved mother went up to God."[1] One of Dorothea Grimm's headaches had come on swiftly several days earlier. The pain in her head was followed by fever, and an infection developed in her lungs. The doctor applied several leeches to her breast, Jacob reported, but Dorothea knew she was dying. Only four weeks earlier, Henriette had visited in Kassel; but, upon her sister's departure back to Gotha, Dorothea was assailed by the thought that she would not be able to see her way through the sadness of their separation. The night before she died, she called all the children to her bedside to bid them farewell. "We are in the most hopeless, inconsolable state and don't know how to help ourselves," Jacob told his aunt. "I cannot write any further. God must comfort us and you. Your Christianity will not abandon you."[2]

Jacob had to find employment quickly. Only days after his mother's death, he was miraculously offered the position of private librarian to King Jerôme. At a starting salary of 2,000 francs, he didn't hesitate to accept. It was certainly enough to support all the siblings. But serving under the Westphalian crown proved to be demoralizing, and Jacob made a point of never attending Jerôme's lavish celebrations or other social gatherings. He was expected to powder his hair and wear it tied back in a ponytail to work, a protocol he found loathsome, and he detested even more having to "stick [him]self into a stiff uniform" styled in the French manner, and then complete the outfit with a cumbersome hat and dagger. "You would have to try it [yourself]," he wrote to Arnim, "to believe how tied down one is with all the formality. There is no feeling of dedication or safety. I know of no one among my superiors who fills me with respect and whom I esteem. . . . It sometimes weighs upon my heart, which is only consoled by the thought that I must earn money for myself and my siblings."[3]

The lack of safety Jacob felt probably had to do with Jerôme's despicable secret police, who "eavesdropped on everything."[4] During the French occupation, the mail was rigorously censored. Wilhelm, too, bemoaned the extreme surveillance, which forced every man to look behind his back "even when he spoke the most innocent words aloud on the street." And "if he stuck a bonbon in his mouth, he didn't throw away the paper that it was wrapped in," because some police spy might "pick it up, hoping to find a secret message inside."[5] Still worse, Jacob's new position had made him a Westphalian citizen by default, meaning that he was included in the lottery for conscription into Napoleon's army. "For eight days, we've lived in the greatest distress and torment," Wilhelm wrote to Henriette that summer.[6] Fortunately, Jacob drew a free number, just escaping the harsh fate of becoming a soldier. Napoleon's Grand Army, known for arduous, fast-paced marches that covered great distances in record time, was now moving westward toward Poland. Ultimately, the army would march all the way to Moscow.

Meanwhile, Ludwig, the youngest of the five Grimm brothers, was now eighteen years old and ready to be formally trained as an artist. With the support of Savigny, Brentano, and Achim and Bettina von Arnim, he left Kassel to study in Heidelberg, and later went to Munich, at his benefactors' expense. Ludwig was fortunate in leaving home after his mother's death, for the mood in the Grimm household had taken a downward turn. Even Wilhelm would later say, and not without jealousy, that of all the siblings, Ludwig was the happiest and most carefree.[7] The red carpet of opportunity had been rolled out before him.

The other brothers, Karl and Ferdinand, were becoming a growing worry for Jacob and Wilhelm. Having dropped out of the lyceum, they insisted they wanted to become writers; but Karl lacked the mind for a literary life, and, though Ferdinand was brilliant, his increasing eccentricity alienated his siblings and even tested the patience of close family friends. Lotte moved in with the Wild family after Dorothea's death. It was supposed to be a temporary stay, but she lingered there for weeks, falling into serious emotional withdrawal. Even her caring friend, Dortchen, could not coax her out of her melancholy.

Though Wilhelm could not bring in a steady income—he would remain unemployed throughout the Westphalian period—he was determined to press forward on the fairy tale project. An opportunity soon presented itself, when Brentano wrote to say that he would be journeying to Allendorf, a town just outside of Marburg, and hoped to meet Wilhelm there. Brentano's wife, Auguste, whom everyone called Fränz, was also staying in Allendorf. Brentano had left her alone there several weeks earlier for a stay of rest, after his family had held a meeting—inviting even Jacob Grimm to participate—and decided that the quarrelsome couple needed a separation from one another to tame the animosity between them. Although Fränz was known to be opinionated and often caused public scenes, her emotional flamboyance vied with that of her husband. "I arrived at the home of these fine people," Brentano described the day he had left Fränz to stay in the house of the Mannels, a family in Allendorf who rented out rooms in their private home, "accompanied by the sound of the coachman's whip" and her "annoying coyness." When it came time for him to leave, "Madame cried, whimpered, felt premonitions of never seeing each other again," Brentano wrote. "I jumped the fence [and] a ghost had disappeared behind me."[8]

Now Brentano wanted Wilhelm to join him in Allendorf, not to see Fränz, but to meet the inexpressibly pleasant Friederike

Mannel, a well-educated young woman who had contributed folk songs to *Des Knaben Wunderhorn*. Friederike ran the guesthouse with her father, a pastor, as a way of raising money to secure her two brothers a formal education. Friederike knew many fairy tales, and Brentano was certain she would be a good source for Jacob and Wilhelm's new project.

In September 1808, Wilhelm agreed to travel to Allendorf to meet up with Brentano, but his visit there did not get off to an auspicious start. His wagon arrived in the village in the middle of the night, when all was dark and silent. Fränz greeted him at the door of the Mannel home and led him to his quarters where, exhausted from the journey, he promptly fell asleep. Early the next morning, Dorothea Grimm appeared to Wilhelm in an eerie dream. As Wilhelm recounted in a letter to Jacob the following day, still chilled by the encounter, his mother had walked across the bedroom and had "reached her hand out to me, as was her habit."[9]

If that wasn't disconcerting enough, Fränz's demeanor was offending Wilhelm to the core. She "has become the most disgusting creature that you can imagine," he carped. "She reads Shakespeare every night and assures [us all] that *Faust* is the very best that . . . Goethe has ever written. She is presumptuous about everything and expresses her opinions in society, but they are incorrect and slanderous. Clemens really can't stand her any more either."[10]

Friederike Mannel, on other hand, was a model of feminine integrity. The moral opposite of Fränz, she was "of such very healthy good-heartedness and friendliness," Wilhelm gushed, "that it does one good to be in her company. She does so without embellishment, which is highly esteemed in this region, and she is truly educated. For example, she understands French. Auguste has been very callous with her. It's infuriating to listen to, and yet [Friederike has] never stopped being gracious toward her. Indeed, such a nature [as hers], which unfolds and moves within its own kindness, is so very charming." There is a hint of the smitten lover in Wilhelm's letter, but, unfortunately for him, Friederike and her feminine accomplishments were already spoken for. "It is very lovely how she speaks so openly about her fiancé and her love [for him]," he mused.[11]

Wilhelm's mission was to speak with Friederike—who had been so forthcoming with Brentano when it came to folk songs—about the fairy tales she remembered or could collect from others. Perhaps she, like the ladies of the Wild family, would become a willing handmaid to the project. Brentano had also begun to collect stories, and there was talk of a collaborative publication with Jacob and Wilhelm. The brothers had certainly taken his cue in turning to women for folklore, but, as it turned out, their approach to collecting material differed dramatically. Jacob and Wilhelm applied their former professor's historical principles to the project, carefully transcribing the stories, as they claimed, word for word; but Brentano made loose notes from tales he heard, then freely adapted them later, adding his own embellishments. Sometimes he arbitrarily changed a story or created an entirely new narrative that, in the brothers' view, was of significant artifice, hardly a document from the ancient past. The result was, in Jacob Grimm's mind, a new literary form that, though inspired by folk tradition, was not a genuine representation of the *Volk.*

Stories such as Brentano's were very different from the simple, organic voice that the Grimms were seeking. They followed the Romantic ideal of *Naturpoesie,* or folk poetry. In a letter to Arnim, Jacob took great pains to explain the distinction:

> Poesie is that which only emanates from the soul and turns into words. Thus it springs continually from a natural drive and innate ability to capture this drive—folk poesie [*Naturpoesie*] stems from the soul of the entire community. What I call cultivated poetry [*Kunstpoesie,* or, in the case of fairy tales, *Kunstmärchen*] stems from the individual. That is why the new poetry names its poets; the old knows none to name. It was not made by one or two or three, but it is the sum of the entire community. We cannot explain how it all came together and was brought forth. But it is not any more mysterious than the manner in which water gathers in a river in order to flow together. . . . The old poesie is completely like the old languages, simple and only rich in itself. In the old language there is nothing but simple words, but they are in themselves so capable of such great reflection and flexibility that the language performs wonders. The new language has lost innocence and has become richer outwardly, but this is through synthesis and coincidence, and therefore it sometimes needs greater preparation in order to express a simple sentence.[12]

Although the brothers disapproved of the poetic license Brentano appeared to be taking in his adaptations, they, too, would alter, especially in later editions of the fairy tales, the transcriptions they had collected from their women friends. But though they edited and cultivated the stories, to use Jacob's words, to suit the tastes of modern, educated readers in the nineteenth century, they nonetheless continued to perpetuate the myth of accurately *preserving* the past by keeping the narrative style simple and the language folksy.

Wilhelm returned home from Allendorf empty handed, but he had established a significant relationship with another potentially dedicated female collaborator. Indeed, over the next two years, Friederike Mannel would add eight tales to the collection. She sent Wilhelm narratives such as "Foundling," a story of two children who escape a demonic cook thanks to their magical powers; a new version of "Child of Mary"; and "Fitcher's Bird,"[13] which possessed similar themes. In this tale, a girl's obedience is tested not by the Virgin Mary but by a villainous *Hexenmeister* (sorcerer) who forbids her to open a certain door, though he gives her the key before conveniently leaving her alone. Naturally, the girl unlocks the door and finds, much to her horror, "a big bloody basin" in the middle of a room containing "dead, chopped up girls, beside which was a woodblock with a gleaming axe." Among the dead virgins in the room, she finds her two long-lost sisters, hacked to pieces. Using the magic powers she has stolen from the sorcerer, the heroine finds her sisters' arms and legs and hands and feet, and pieces their bodies together, bringing them back to life.

Friederike Mannel's contributions exemplify the variety of ways that a story ultimately made its way into the *Children's and Household Fairy Tales*. Some of the stories she sent to Wilhelm were penned in her own hand, others by her father's apprentices, who presumably recorded her stories as she told them. As multiple versions of the same tales surfaced among their growing number of collaborators, the brothers fused segments of stories together in so-called contaminations, so that two, three, even four versions of one story came to represent a Grimm fairy tale for posterity.

Examples of the contamination process include "Child of Mary," as well as "King Thrushbeard,"[14] a story that pitted feminine virtues against feminine vices and, by doing so, provided readers with edifying lessons in proper female behavior. "King Thrushbeard" also tested the boundaries of fantasy and real life when it came to the various relationships of the people who sojourned in the Mannels' guesthouse. The tale is pedantic in its depiction of its heroine's good and evil traits, much in the way that Brentano and Wilhelm Grimm framed Friederike and Fränz in their personal letters. Even the two women's names, when paired together, read like a fairy tale of mythical opposites: *Friederike*, the gracious and conscientious, versus *Fränz*, the sinister and hysterical. In "King Thrushbeard," the heroine, embodying good- and bad-girl roles, starts out as an opinionated, willful princess who poses a challenge to the institution of marriage, just as Fränz Brentano did. Not wanting to marry at all, the princess pokes fun at her suitors' foibles one after another as she rejects their proposals. "One was too fat for her," the story reads. "What a wine barrel!" the princess exclaims. Another was too gangly: "Clumsy and long just isn't my song." The third was too short: "The fat and small have no poise at all." The fourth, too pale: "Why, he's white as death!"

The fifth, too red: "Just like a rooster!" And the sixth, well, he just wasn't straight enough: "He's like green wood, drying behind the oven!"

The princess makes the most fun of a king with a crooked chin. "Ay!" she calls and laughs, "his chin looks like a thrush's beak." But when her father sees that his daughter does nothing but scorn all the bachelors who have assembled there before her, he becomes angry and swears that she will take as her husband the very next beggar who comes to their door. Just then a poor musician happens by, and the princess must leave the castle with him. She follows her husband to their new home, a shack in the woods, where she fails miserably at the simplest of household chores: lighting a fire, cooking food, weaving baskets, and spinning. "You see, you're good for nothing," her husband scolds her, complaining how poorly he's done by marrying such a useless woman. In time, our heroine ends up as a scullery maid in a castle where she must help the cook and perform the miserable grunt work. Hiding two little pots in each of her pockets, she fills them with scraps from the kitchen and brings them home each night to her husband. It is their only food.

One day, there is a wedding at the castle. The young woman stands at the entrance to the ballroom, admiring the festivities. "As the lights were being lit," the story reads, "and as one person more beautiful than the next entered, and as everything was full of magnificence and splendor, she thought with a sad heart of her fate and cursed the pride and arrogance that had demeaned her and thrust her into such great poverty." The smells of the fine dishes fill her senses, but the other servants toss her mere crumbs, which she adds to the soup she has scrounged for her little pots.

Then the king who is to be wed appears. He is wearing velvet and silk and golden chains hang from his neck. Enchanted by the lovely young woman standing in the doorway, he takes her by the hand and asks her to dance. She is terrified, for she sees that it is King Thrushbeard, the man whom she had once rejected in mockery. When he pulls her out into the ballroom, her little pots of food fall out of her apron, spilling soup and scattering crumbs everywhere. Laughter fills the room, and all the fine guests deride her. The girl is so ashamed that she wishes to be "a thousand fathoms below the earth." She tries to flee, but King Thrushbeard chases her and brings her back. He tells her not to fear and reveals to her that, all along, he has been living in disguise as the poor musician, posing as her husband. "All of this has happened to bend your pride and to punish you for your arrogance," he chastises her. The girl cries bitterly and confesses: "I did you a great injustice and am not worthy of being your wife." But her shame and public confession are just what's required for her to join the social fold once more, not to mention the proper institution of marriage, which she had so arrogantly rejected.

In Wilhelm Grimm's eyes, Friederike Mannel was impeccably good, and a most acceptable addition to the fairy tale project. Her letters to him gushed with devotion, almost in a wifely way. "Speaking with you," she wrote to him shortly after his departure from Allendorf, "has become such sweet custom to me that I must say a few words this evening, while sitting at the big table, no matter how late it is. . . . I'm still sad that you have left. I still find myself incapable of feeling truly cheerful. When you left me, my right eye cried. It cries much more easily than the other [eye], but not too easily." Then Friederike told Wilhelm that she hadn't moved the special chair that he had used during his stay from its place. "Good night Mr. Grimm," she closed the letter, and then she apologized for her poor handwriting: "My scribbles look unwieldy, I'm sure, but that doesn't matter. Sleep well my dear!"[15]

One month later, Friederike reported that Brentano had returned to Allendorf to pick up Fränz and that the couple had traveled to Landshut together. She also included two fairy tales with the correspondence. Friederike tended to make mention of her contributions to the project as an afterthought in her letters. Perhaps it would have been too immodest of her to call attention to her labors, or to parade them before her correspondent, a man of high learning. In assuming the role of ever patient and forgiving friend, she spent far more time writing about Fränz than about the fairy tales. "Ach," she lamented in another letter to Wilhelm in the winter of 1809, Fränz "is very unhappy. Each day she becomes more dear to me in her immeasurable suffering."[16]

Periodically, Fränz would return to Allendorf for another "rest," and Friederike dutifully relayed the news to Wilhelm. "We all received Auguste joyfully and happily," she wrote with false optimism on one such occasion in an effort to cover up her own father's hatred for Brentano's wife. "We all love her, especially me. . . . And you should see her now! So friendly, so

participatory. No woman could be so devoted to us in our relations." But Friederike was quick to qualify herself. "Do not believe that with this I wish to judge you and Brentano. . . . You
and he have your [own] views."[17]

Pejoratives about Fränz flowed readily from the pens of
males who knew her. In a letter to his Aunt Henriette, Wilhelm
referred to her as "Brentano's godless wife,"[18] and Friederike's
father, Pastor Mannel, called her a "pest" and a "monstrosity"[19]
who was "strong in her irony."[20] Like the bad wife in "King
Thrushbeard," Fränz Brentano was certainly not "worthy" in
many of her male peers' eyes. There is strong evidence that she
suffered from profound depression, and she attempted to take
her own life at various times during her marriage with Brentano.
Before the first year of their life together as husband and wife
had passed, Brentano no longer lived with Fränz in any regular
fashion. He left her instead at the Mannels' boarding house and
other such establishments for long periods. By 1810, they were
formally divorced. Fränz was only nineteen years old.

Meanwhile, Friederike married, and Wilhelm continued his
correspondence with her. Brentano, he wrote, giving Friederike
news of his friend's divorce, was "finally liberated from his hard
luck that [had] gripped his heart so strongly, every day, like a
goblin."[21] Though the couple was no longer together, Wilhelm
would still encounter Fränz from time to time in public and at
social gatherings. On one occasion, she turned up in Kassel "on
horseback in men's clothing."[20] Then he found her again in
Berlin, dressed in the same reprehensible fashion, where she was
so bold as to eat at "public tables like that in the city, where

many know her."²³ He saw "her infamous face" seated in the loge next to his in the theater. "I was frightened," he wrote to Friederike, "for it was as if a heavy hand waved across [Fränz's face], causing all her features to turn downward." When he heard of the woman's plans to marry again, he quickly penned a letter to Friederike. "You must send me news about it," he gossiped, adding that she should especially tell him "who the unlucky man is." Fränz, Wilhelm was certain, would surely lead the fellow "into the hell of April."²⁴ Indeed, she did marry again, and she had children, too, but in 1832, at the age of forty-one, she drowned herself in the Main River in Frankfurt.

Fränz Brentano, or Auguste Bußman, as she was called before her unhappy life with Brentano, was a woman at odds with her time. Her unfortunate life shows that the good-girl/bad-girl dyad was embedded in the fairy tales for a reason: It was a reflection of the culture at large. Meanwhile, Jacob and Wilhelm were beginning to see that Friederike Mannel was a diligent handmaid. In all her pliancy and willingness to serve, she was a wife of sorts, the kind of "worthy" wife the heroine of "King Thrushbeard" becomes at the end of the story, the kind of devoted partner the brothers needed to help carry out their daunting fairy tale project.

5

THE SIX SWANS

On December 8, 1808, Achim von Arnim wrote to Clemens Brentano that he was visiting in Kassel and "residing very comfortably" with the Grimm family. "You know them," he sang their praises, "they're the most sincere people in the world." But in spite of the hospitality he was offered in Jacob and Wilhelm's modest home, Arnim was unsettled by the astonishing discord he had discovered among the Grimm siblings. Tensions were high. Wilhelm's health had vividly degenerated, and Arnim was convinced that Jacob, now twenty-four years old, was far too soft and yielding to be the patriarch of a household. Ferdinand, for example, wasn't suited for the intellectual life, and Arnim felt it was time for the family to accept that he should learn a trade. As for Lotte, she should be packed off to "a strict boarding house," Arnim complained, because she took "no interest whatsoever in domesticity."[1]

Jacob and Wilhelm couldn't have agreed more with Arnim's sentiments concerning Lotte. Now that Dorothea Grimm was gone, it was only natural that she should bear the brunt of the family's routine domestic needs. But minding the washing, cooking, sewing, and cleaning for four men—Ludwig was the only brother living out of the house at the time—amounted to never-ending toil, particularly as she could employ only one reluctant woman servant to assist her. Ferdinand was often irritable and loafed around the house all day, which didn't help matters, and Karl plugged away at his measly job at the bank, returning home in low spirits every evening. All the while, Jacob and Wilhelm worked long hours sequestered away together in their shared study, taking breaks only for meals, strolls, and afternoon coffee. And naturally they expected Lotte to keep up with their every need.

Although Lotte had returned home after living with the Wilds for a brief period, the new household requirements heaped upon her made going across the street to see her friends more and more attractive. The Grimms' house became very untidy, and the linens went unwashed. Meals, no longer a shared family event, were taken erratically. Upon hearing about this state of affairs, Aunt Zimmer was dismayed. "Dear Lotte, you're not a child any more. You are 15 years old, and you can accomplish very much with the housekeeping without doing harm to your body," she sternly wrote from Gotha. "For God's sake, see to it that it doesn't look dirty or untidy" and "pay special attention to the undergarments."[2]

The Grimm children had become lost souls, each in his or her own fashion. By spring of 1809, Wilhelm was growing frighteningly short of breath, and his heart pounded in anxious, irregular beats. The condition had become so terrifying to him that, after great consternation over leaving Jacob alone, he broke down and decided to journey to a special clinic in Halle to seek out the help of Dr. Reil, a physician widely known for his success at treating heart ailments. Except for the occasional brief visit to places such as Allendorf, Wilhelm had never been away from Kassel for extended periods and the intensive research around which he and Jacob had built their daily lives. Jacob, never having been the one left behind, did not disguise his disapproval of the journey, even though the urgency of Wilhelm's condition demanded that he seek medical attention.

In a family accustomed to always doing without, Wilhelm naturally felt guilty on the day of his departure. Once he was on the road, however, he surprised himself and noted that he felt "absolutely fine during the entire trip," even though he hadn't slept for several nights in a row.[3] Distancing himself from Kassel, not to mention from his grieving siblings, was already having a beneficial effect upon his health. The journey took him through Gotha, where he visited Henriette. His coach arrived in the city very early in the morning, and he found his aunt still in bed and very pleased and surprised to see him, even though Wilhelm could stay with her only for an hour. Henriette, he wrote to Jacob, was living "very beautifully, brightly, sweetly, almost elegantly" in her new quarters, and the "needle-work from Lotte brought her much joy." In her bedroom above her bed, she had hung a painting of the Christ head. "It's a poor image," he concluded, "but lovely because of her pious sentiment."[4] That day, nephew and aunt had a good talk together, especially about the war. In the face of Napoleon's hold on Europe and the successive victories that had exalted his Grand Army to mythic proportion, it was doubtful whether Aunt Zimmer would ever return to Kassel.

When it was time for his coach to leave, Wilhelm bid Henriette farewell with a heavy heart, not knowing when he'd see his dear aunt again. His journey took him through Erfurt, and then Weimar, the home of Goethe. As he proceeded, he saw more and more traces of the war. One night, at around midnight, he wrote to Jacob, his coach had passed through the infamous battlefields of Auerstädt, where, three years earlier, 20,000 soldiers had lost their lives in the decisive battle that had forced Henriette, as well as their regent, Wilhelm I, to evacuate Kassel. The countless graves he saw illuminated in the eerie moonlight made an unforgettable impression on Wilhelm.

But the death fields of Auerstädt were only a prologue to the sad and peculiar things that would happen to him in Halle. "A few days ago, I spoke with Reil," he wrote to Jacob on April 1, 1809, after his first consultation with the doctor. Wilhelm then proceeded to describe the visit with modest Protestant embarrassment: "He came up to my room. I had to show him my entire chest and body, which he observed for a long time. He said it is a rare, abnormal condition in my heart, which was working and beating under heavy pressure."[5] The question Reil was faced with, Wilhelm told Jacob, was how these external manifestations could be explained internally.

To begin treatment, Reil had prescribed a balm, which Wilhelm was to apply to his heart in a compress several times a day. The cure—he delicately broke the news to Jacob—would require several months of treatment. "Not that I believe I can completely regain my health," he added. At most, Wilhelm hoped that Reil might offer him "some improvement and relief." He also felt compelled to divulge a secret to his brother that he had been keeping for a long time. For years, Wilhelm confessed, he had felt "responsible" for "not having tried everything to release myself from this real fear of death."[6] He knew Jacob would take this news with difficulty. The cost of the treatments, let alone room and board, was not something the family could afford, and although Wilhelm was bringing in some honoraria for reviews and essays he had written, he knew much of the burden would fall on Jacob. Fortunately, Aunt Henriette, in her undying generosity, had offered to assist him with some of the costs when he visited her in Gotha. Filled with guilt and desperately seeking ways to cut expenses, Wilhelm rented a room the size of a matchbox and took meals with some acquaintances in Halle who were "in desperate straits," just as he was. "It's a frugal table," he wrote to Jacob. Then, closing the letter, he begged his brother not to think that he wished in being there, "to engage in pleasures."[7] Certainly the scrimping and the worry didn't help Wilhelm's convalescence.

Though Jacob was feeling remorse for having opposed his brother's journey to Halle, he could not contain his complex emotions about what promised to be a protracted absence from

Kassel. Two weeks had passed since Wilhelm's departure. It "naturally makes me sad," he wrote glumly on April 15 in reply to his brother's letter. "I'm living much more silently and distraught than you are in Halle."[8]

Wilhelm tried to settle into his new solitude. He passed the time by reading and writing all alone in his tiny room each day, but it was unusual to work in this fashion, without his brother's abiding intellectual company. The fairy tale project was suffering. In another letter home, Wilhelm reported that he had asked around Halle for stories, but all he had been able to elicit from acquaintances there was a disappointing copy of 1001 Nights. "No one knows the real thing," he complained.[9] After their initial success at collecting stories from Friederike Mannel and the Wild sisters, the anthology seemed to be losing ground, and each day the treatments with Reil became more tedious and time consuming. The doctor introduced new regimens that limited Wilhelm's attention for work. He found himself charting his days out by the clock, swallowing pills, applying compresses, and taking multiple baths of various depths and temperatures at specified intervals throughout the day.

"In the morning, when I get up at seven thirty," he wearily described, "I rub down my neck with a strong black, mercurial salve. After that, I wash my heart with spirits. At 9 o'clock I take a powder that is extremely repulsive."[10] The medicament made Wilhelm so nauseous that, half an hour later, he was forced to take a bitter essence to restore his stomach and appetite. This regimen continued into the afternoons and evenings, severely compromising his ability to study and read.

At one point, Reil even introduced a bizarre form of shock therapy. With chains hung upon his neck and body, Wilhelm was hooked up to a "magnificently large machine made of mahogany," whereupon he was brought into contact with electricity. The current coursed through his body, yet he felt nothing, except for a bit of uneasiness. "But if someone touches me, or even my jacket," he added, "strong sparks fly up and crackle."[11] On particularly hot days, the treatment was so strong that blisters emerged where the conductors had touched his skin. Wilhelm was also having many vivid dreams: "Great strange dreams that are linked to one another," he wrote, darkly adding that nearly all of them had a sad ending, unlike the traditional, optimistic "happy ending" of so many of the fairy tales the brothers had been collecting.[12]

In his isolation, Wilhelm was falling into melancholy, something his mother had always been prone to, also. But life at home in Kassel was no better for the rest of his mourning siblings. Dorothea Grimm had left a gaping hole in their hearts, and there was no easy way to fill it. "I think of our brothers with disappointment," Wilhelm confided to Jacob in another gloomy letter. "It is so clear to me that in Ferdinand's case, severity, indeed even a certain force, is called for." Ferdinand was twenty-one years old now, and he was heading straight for disaster, Wilhelm thought. If he continued his life of idleness for ten more years, he would surely turn into "an imbecile." As for Karl, aged twenty-two, he "grasped, almost blindly, at anyone in whom he might hope to find a crutch" and suffered from an "internal lack of solace."[13] Ludwig, the youngest brother, though he was hardworking and talented, grieved Wilhelm by the extreme material sacrifices he was forced to make in order to train as an artist.

Then Wilhelm got around to their sister. "If I think of our brothers with pain, then I think of Lotte with shyness and fear because the stone upon her heart is getting heavier and heavier, to the point that mercy, love, and rage can no longer touch it. Have you not noticed, when she is at events that are meant to be pleasures, she is never joyful?" Lotte, at the age of sixteen, registered few emotions other than boredom and sullenness.

Lotte Grimm's solitary role as the only girl in a family of many brothers showed fascinating parallels with "The Six Swans,"[14] a story her friend Dortchen Wild contributed to the fairy tale anthology. It tells of a girl whose six brothers fall prey to an evil spell, cast by their stepmother, that transforms them all into swans. Fearing that her stepmother might harm her, too, and sorrowful about her six brothers' enchantment, the girl runs away from home without telling her father. For one night and one day, the heroine walks alone through the forest. Lotte Grimm walked into a similar metaphoric forest of aloneness after her mother died. The suddenness of the domestic expectations forced upon her came from brothers who seemed to have transformed overnight in their love for her, as if some evil curse had overtaken them. They no longer related to their sister as a fellow sibling; instead, they now saw her as little more than their domestic servant.

In the same way that Lotte found safe haven from the demands of her home life in the Wild household, the heroine of "The Six Swans" discovers a small cottage on her journey through the dark forest. Stepping inside the cottage, the girl finds a room with six small beds in it. Denying her own need for comfort, she crawls beneath one of the beds and falls asleep. Suddenly, six swans come flying in through the window and land on the floor. As they do so, the magnificent birds begin blowing on one another until all their feathers fall off, like a robe slipping from a body. Then, amazingly, the swans turn into six young princes. They are the girl's long-lost brothers. Overjoyed, she crawls out from under the bed to surprise and greet them. The brothers are happy to see her, but they admonish their sister to leave the cottage immediately, for it belongs to dangerous robbers, and she could be discovered. The princes also reveal to her that under the evil curse placed upon them, they will remain in human form only for fifteen minutes before they turn back into swans again. This phenomenon, they say, happens each evening right at sunset.

"If you want to save us," the brothers tell their sister, "you must sew six small shirts made of aster flowers." All the while, the girl may not speak, and she may not laugh; otherwise, her chore would be performed in vain. With that, the princes' moment of humanness is over. Having imparted their requirements of their sister, they turn back into swans and fly away.

The heroine of the story sets to work immediately. The very next day, she gathers up the necessary flowers in the forest, then perches herself high in a tree where, saying "not one word" and "never laughing," she "only [sees] to her labors." Nothing can distract this girl from her purpose, not even a handsome prince traveling through the forest with his hunting party. The men see her sitting high up in the tall tree and call to her, but she keeps her vow of silence and doesn't respond. When they beg her to come down, she ignores them. When they press her again, she tries to fob them off by removing her gold necklace and tossing it down. Still, they persist, so she throws down her belt, then her stockings, and then "everything," the story tells us, until all she is wearing is "a little smock," a symbol of her material sacrifice in the name of her brothers.

Undeterred by the strange girl's stubbornness, the prince orders his huntsmen to climb the tree and bring her down. When he beholds her for the first time, her shining beauty stuns him. Then, he wraps the half-naked girl in his cape, scoops her up onto his horse, and brings her home to the castle. "So what if she was mute," the story tells us. "He loved her with all his heart, and he married her."

The familiar notion that silence denotes feminine goodness runs deep in "The Six Swans." But Lotte Grimm, though she was a mute figure in a house of many brothers, expressed a silence that was far different from that of the heroine of the story. Lotte's silence was a reticence that perplexed and outraged Jacob and Wilhelm. By refusing to replace their mother as the family nurturer, who, by early-nineteenth-century European standards, was seamlessly equated with domestic fastidiousness, she was not holding to her most critical feminine responsibility.

Though Lotte's stony moods were aggravating, Jacob could also see that his sister was suffering and that her only solace seemed to be with her friends across the street. So the brothers agreed to let her go to Marburg to visit Gretchen Wild, who had recently married and moved there with her husband. Perhaps the visit would do their sister some good, they reasoned, and it was comforting to think of her residing in the very haunts of their former university town. But Jacob had some reservations, too. On several occasions, he wrote to Wilhelm in Halle, he had overheard Lisette Wild making remarks that confirmed for him what he had already assumed, namely, "a certain hardness and coldness in Gretchen's nature."[15] The trip could backfire, for Gretchen might end up exerting a negative influence on a sister who had already become too cold of heart.

As it turned out, Lotte's trip to Marburg was not intended solely for her benefit. Jacob and Wilhelm also hoped to enlist their sister in the fairy tale collecting by having her transcribe stories from the legendary "fairy tale lady of Marburg," an old woman whom Brentano had once met and raved about. Apparently, this gifted storyteller had told him several excellent stories, but Brentano only "wrote down single words and falsely believed that he wouldn't forget how it went," Wilhelm complained. Wilhelm also lamented that Brentano couldn't return to Marburg himself to see the woman again. Because the town was in such close proximity to Allendorf, he was afraid of being ambushed by Fränz, his hysterical wife.[16]

Much to Jacob and Wilhelm's dismay, Lotte cut off nearly all communication when she arrived in Marburg. Letters to her went unanswered, even Ferdinand's, with whom Lotte had the most empathetic relationship. Ferdinand, always in conflict with his older brothers, saw Lotte as his only ally in the family and was extremely dependent upon her emotionally. "Oh, Lotte," he pleaded in a letter to Marburg, "why have you not written to me? Oh, why have you not told me how you are doing? . . . Don't be so free of kindness or love."[17]

Lotte ended up staying in Marburg weeks longer than her brothers had originally allowed for. Together with Gretchen, she walked the steep, stone roads that connected the lovely town into a delicate web of paths to and from the markets they shopped, the homes of friends they visited, and the church they attended. Lotte had never known such freedom as she strolled past the buildings of the university and the homes of erudite professors under whom Jacob and Wilhelm had studied when, as young men, they had experienced their first taste of independence from home. Yet Lotte had little connection with these scholars and their publications, just as she had little connection with the fairy tale project. Although her closest female friends had proved to be devoted participants, Lotte failed to contribute even one story. Her resentment was strong. Jacob and Wilhelm had their privileged status as educated men of letters to make up for whatever material lack the family suffered, but Lotte had nothing. She faced this painful fact every day in a house of brothers who acknowledged her for little more than her utilitarian purposes.

By August, Wilhelm's spirits began to lift a little. His treatments with Reil were finally ending, and Brentano had also paid him an unexpected visit, arriving in Halle pining and thin from his separation from Fränz and making dramatic claims that he would "never take her again."[18] Brentano also shared his plans to publish an anthology of fairy tales and asked Wilhelm for a copy of the brothers' collection. Jacob felt it wouldn't hurt to give the manuscript to their friend, convinced as he was that Brentano would approach the tales "differently than what [the brothers had] in mind."[19] Taking care not to give their wayward friend the only copy they possessed, Jacob and Wilhelm went to great pains in producing a full transcription of the manuscript, which now stood at the admirable count of forty-nine stories.

Seeing Wilhelm in better health than he had ever known him before, Brentano urged his friend to join him as his guest on a trip to Berlin, where they could stay with Arnim. At this news of Wilhelm's delay in returning home, Jacob's spirits sank. Lotte had finally returned from Marburg, but her company only afflicted him and drew his sad thoughts to his mother. In a reminiscing letter to Wilhelm, he wrote of their school vacations as boys when, every year, they had gone to see Dorothea in Steinau. But the month always went by so quickly, and their mother cried so bitterly when they departed. "Ach," Jacob lamented, "if only she were still alive. Since her death, our home has become distressing because not one of us is connected to the other, and there is no longer any routine . . . I am certain that if a person lives moderately and quietly, as we do, then order and cleanliness are the priority," Jacob wrote in criticism of Lotte's housekeeping again, and added that the Wild's apothecary, where their sister spent most of her time, was repulsive to him.[20]

After visiting Gretchen in Marburg, Lotte had returned to Kassel empty-handed, that is, with no stories to add to the anthology. Though she had visited the fairy tale lady of Marburg, she "didn't deal with the woman properly or take her into her confidence," Wilhelm complained.[21] In truth, however, the old woman, who was employed at a hospital, where Lotte went to see her, was afraid to tell the tales aloud for fear that others working there would deride her for speaking nonsense and being ridiculous. It's likely that she was embarrassed when she learned that male scholars would be scrutinizing the stories she told.[22]

In the same letter to Jacob, Wilhelm also took Gretchen Wild to task about their failing project. She was no longer willing to participate in the collecting, he complained, because she was "concerned with nothing but her husband, and [was] afraid, like most females, about her writing mistakes."[23] The competition with Brentano, even if the brothers knew they approached the stories with a far different editorial philosophy, was making Wilhelm feel all the more desperate about finding ways of reinvigorating the process. Still, more bad news was to come: Friederike Mannel also dropped out, compounding the brothers' frustration. Friederike had discovered that the demands of her marriage, what with the domestic chores and her husband's comforts to think about, left her no time for transcribing stories.

In the tale of "The Six Swans," the heroine, after suffering much public derision for her inexplicable silence, eventually saves her six brothers from the evil spell that was cast upon them. But before they are saved, her silence gets her into trouble. The girl is accused of killing her own newborn children and cannot defend herself against the accusation. As in "Child of Mary," she is sentenced to burn at the stake, but she has the foresight, when she is taken to her execution, to bring the little sweaters she has knitted from aster petals. They are nearly all finished. Only one is missing a sleeve. Then, just as the fire is being lit at her feet, the six swans come swooping down from the sky. As they fly past the girl, she tosses the small sweaters onto each of their bodies, whereupon the birds instantly turn into princes. The spell is broken, and the story ends happily, though one of the brothers—the one wearing the sleeveless sweater—is not completely restored to humanness. In place of an arm, he must live with one swan's wing forever protruding from his back, a dark reminder of the misfortune that had torn their family asunder.

All of Lotte Grimm's brothers seemed to wear a symbolic swan's wing on their own backs. Each had some deficit that made him human, and sometimes, from Lotte's perspective, inhuman, too. "She has it too good and always follows her own will," Jacob complained to Wilhelm in another angry letter as the fairy tale project continued to languish. "But that is the principal result of mother's death, and it won't change."[24]

6

THE MAIDEN WITH NO HANDS

WHILE WILHELM WAS IN BERLIN WITH BRENTANO and Arnim, Jacob, much to his own surprise, discovered a new source of fairy tales right in Kassel. The situation was uncanny. Through a mutual friend, he was introduced to the Hassenpflugs, a prominent family of the city that was well endowed with daughters. Typical of Jacob's ever-critical opinion of Kassel's provincialism, he found these sisters—Susette, Jeanette, Marie, and Amalia—to be "likable enough," but, more important, he wrote to Wilhelm with a bit of the mercenary in his tone, the young women had shared several "entirely new" stories with him, unlike any others the brothers had transcribed to date. What was more, they had promised that "more would be remembered and gathered."[1]

It was the autumn of 1809. Wilhelm had been away for six months, but the discovery of the Hassenpflugs gave the brothers a glimmer of hope for their anthology. These ladies were like a fairy tale think tank, and when Wilhelm returned home in December that year from his convalescence, the young women soon became steady members of the reading circle that met each week in the Grimm home. The salon had become a center for gatherings of the young, educated middle class of Kassel. It brought Lotte Grimm and the women of the Wild and Hassenpflug families together, and meaningful friendships developed around their delight in telling and remembering stories.

Johannes Hassenpflug, the father of the four daughters and one son, held the esteemed political office of Governmental President of Hesse and provided very well for his children. Of the girls, Susette Hassenpflug contributed the least number of stories to the Grimm collection, if any at all. Many titles added by the sisters were group efforts, and thus Susette's potential participation remains a bit of a mystery. She married and moved out of the house the same year the brothers began associating with her family.

Jeanette, the second eldest, was a significant collaborator. Only a few years younger than Jacob and Wilhelm—she was nineteen when she began telling stories to the Grimms—Jeanette was admired by everyone in the reading circle for her dramatic narrations. Like Jacob and Wilhelm, she had been born in Hanau, where her father was once the mayor of the city before her family moved to Kassel. Jeanette brought several new titles to the Grimms' collection, such as "Puss in Boots," the story of a clever talking cat who helps a poor miller win a tremendous fortune, a beautiful queen, and a kingdom to call his own. She also told "Hurleburlebutz," the tale of a dwarf who uncovers the secret identity of a princess the moment she refuses, because she is royal, to pick the lice from his hair. But because the princess's father has promised the girl in marriage to the cunning dwarf, she is forced into wedlock against her will. Fortunately for the princess, she manages to break a spell that was cast upon the dwarf, and so he turns into a handsome prince. Two other tales Jeanette gave the brothers were, "The Twelve Huntsmen," a harsh lesson about the father's authority over his progeny when it comes to marriage, and "Okerlo," which tells of a prince and princess who, stranded on an island of cannibals, manage to escape certain death by wearing a pair of magic "seven-mile boots," which carry them one mile for every step they take. In the end, they, too, enjoy a happy marriage. Indeed, it seems the plot of "boy meets girl" had pervaded the fairy tale genre, and for Jeanette, and other young, unwed women of the age, the inevitable happy ending held out a sign of hope.

One of the most peculiar stories Jeanette Hassenpflug ever told was called "On the Despicable Spinning of Flax,"[2] a paradoxical narrative about women's toil and women's beauty. The story opens with a king who "loves nothing more in the world than the spinning of flax," particularly when females are doing the spinning. He therefore orders his wife and two daughters to spin enough flax to fill a very large trunk; he further demands that they finish this colossal chore before he returns home from a journey. When the young princesses see the crushing work that lies before them, they cry to their mother: "We'll be sitting here all day long [and] won't be allowed to get up even once." The potential oppressiveness of women's confinement lace the narrative with dark undercurrents.

The queen, however, consoles her daughters with a brilliant plan. She calls for three especially ugly maids to do the work for them. The first maid, we learn, has a lower lip that is so large it droops all the way down to her chin. The second has a pointer finger that is so thick and wide that three more fingers could be made from it. And the third has a clubfoot the size of "a kitchen cutting board." The queen commands the three strange crones to spin the flax, and they set to work immediately.

Upon arriving home from his journey, the king's ears perk up when he hears "the grating of the spinning wheel" emanating from his castle. The sound fills him with joy. Wanting to heap praises upon his hardworking daughters, he rushes in to see them, but he is startled to find the three foul maids sitting at the spinning wheels. Appalled, he approaches the first woman and asks her where on earth she got her disgusting lip: "From licking! From licking!" she replies matter-of-factly, and then returns to her tedious chores. When he asks the second where she got her "fat, fat finger," the woman tells him that she got it "from twisting thread, from twisting thread." Finally, he approaches the third ugly maid and asks about her extremely corpulent foot: "From pedaling, from pedaling!" she exclaims. The classic conflict of the patriarch is revealed here. He likes the idea of laboring women in his household because toil keeps them in their place. But hard work also damages feminine beauty. Deciding that it is far worse a fate to have ugly women in his castle, the king orders his wife and daughters never to touch a spinning wheel again as long as they live. And so the king releases them forever, the story tells us, "from this torment."

This tale must have spawned wistful sighs from many a young female listener who recognized the harsh message in it: As women, their beauty was perhaps their only asset. But what if a girl wasn't beautiful? Jeanette Hassenpflug's little sister, Amalia, was only nine years old when she met Jacob and Wilhelm, and though she didn't contribute stories until she was older, her sister Jeanette's strange tale of the spinning crones must have captured her attention. Amalia Hassenpflug, like the ugly maids in the story, was not blessed with beauty. Her nose was slightly crooked and her eyes were crossed. Yet, even as a young girl, her intelligence was striking and her memory particularly well suited for retelling fairy tales.

When Jacob and Wilhelm first met Malchen, as Amalia was sometimes nicknamed, she was something of a tomboy and more disposed toward playing with boys than with other girls. She showed no interest whatsoever in dolls, and she preferred acting out fairy tale plots with her brother Ludwig, taking on the role of a knight or a prince in the service of a damsel in distress, who was generally played by one of her older sisters. Malchen became very close to Lotte Grimm and Dortchen Wild through the fairy tale project. The types of narratives she added to the Grimms' anthology were scary ghost stories, such as "The

Strange Feast," a tale about a murderous blood sausage that deceptively attempts to kill a liver sausage, and "The Godfather," a dark and gory tale about a poor man who is granted the power of seeing death before it descends on other people.

If Malchen Hassenpflug was crone-like, then her older sister Marie, with her delicate features, dark hair and eyes, and slender lips, was the striking beauty of the family. Marie gave the brothers Grimm the most renowned stories the *Children's and Household Fairy Tales* would ever know. Of the more than forty fairy tales contributed by the Hassenpflug household to the collection, twenty alone are attributed to Marie. She was an exceedingly prolific storyteller, and her entrée into the project came at a moment when Jacob and Wilhelm were grappling with questions about the nature of the fairy tale genre. Marie's additions of such classics as "Sleeping Beauty" and "Red Riding Hood" inspired the brothers in their historical research and caused them to view folklore in ever more international terms.

Coming into contact with the Grimms and the stimulating reading circle changed Marie Hassenpflug's life. Ever since she was a young girl, she had been exceedingly withdrawn and sickly, especially after she had suffered from a seizure-like episode when a momentary unconsciousness befell her and she lost the use of her limbs. Though she regained movement, the family always felt that the mysterious faint had rendered Marie especially receptive to fairy tales. It was as if storytelling had compensated for the burden of her poor health. In this way, Marie had much in common with Wilhelm Grimm, whose own mystifying heart ailment acted like a dark muse to his strong poetic imagination.

The moment Marie met Jacob and Wilhelm and began telling them stories, her intellectual path soared beyond the convention for a woman of the era. Knowing these scholar brothers gave her a first taste of inspiration, and her passion for poetry, for Goethe, and for the history of literature suddenly took flight. Soon, fairy tales and old German medieval epics were all she could talk about; they became a constant object of conversation in the Hassenpflug home, as Marie's enthusiasm infected all the other siblings of the household.

In March 1811, Marie submitted a remarkable story to the Grimm anthology titled "The Maiden with No Hands."[3] It is a tale of a girl's self-sacrificing obedience to her father, which in turn leads her to her own sorrowful victimization. The story opens with a miller who is so poor that he has nothing but his mill and the great apple tree standing behind it. One day, the miller must go into the forest to gather wood. While he is there, an old man approaches him and asks, "Why are you so tormented? I will make you rich. In exchange, turn what's standing behind your mill over to me. I will come to fetch it in three years' time." Thinking the old man wants nothing more than his apple tree, the miller readily makes the pact. When he goes home, he finds his wife waiting for him. "Miller," she exclaims, "where did the great treasure that suddenly filled our house with trunks and boxes come from?" The miller proudly tells his wife about the clever trade he made with the stranger in the woods. "Ach, husband," she cries out, "this can only lead to evil. That old man was the devil, and he was talking about our daughter who happened to be sweeping up behind the mill."

Three years pass, and the devil comes to collect the miller's daughter; but, clever girl, she has drawn a protective ring around herself with chalk and has thoroughly washed herself. Thus, she prevents the demon from laying his hands on her. Enraged by the girl's treachery, the devil tells the miller not to allow his daughter to bathe, so that he may have power over her. A dirty girl, the story teaches, falls easy prey to evil deceits. Fearing for his own safety, the miller selfishly refuses his daughter water to bathe in, but the imperiled girl is in such despair that she "cries into her hands and washes herself in her own tears, making herself "pure" and invincible in the face of the devil's powers.

Seeing that he has only one more chance at possessing the maiden's soul—good and bad luck, as we know, always comes in threes—the devil orders the miller to chop off his daughter's hands. Terrified, the miller wails, "How could I chop the hands off of my own dear child?" He refuses to commit such a terrible crime. But the devil threatens to take his soul if he doesn't obey. The selfish man reconsiders and decides that sacrificing his daughter isn't such a bad idea after all. In many of the Grimms' fairy tales, a father's authority lords above all else. No matter how unjust his own actions might appear to be, they are always interpreted as serving some higher purpose.

"My child," the miller pleads with his daughter, "the devil will get me if I don't chop off both your hands. I promised this to him. I beg you for forgiveness."

"Father," the maiden replies, "do as you please with me." With that, she bravely holds out her hands and allows her father to chop them off.

In the Middle Ages, stories of incest and innocent virgins stalked by their own fathers were commonplace, and although nineteenth-century German propriety censored explicit references to such hideous acts of sexual violence, its legacy still lurked implicitly in such tales as "The Maiden with No Hands," in which the self-sacrificing virgin becomes the victim of her father's egotism.[4] When the devil comes for the maiden the third time, again he fails to capture her soul because, the story tells us, she cries so long and so hard "all over her stumps" that she washes herself completely pure.

Now that our heroine has safely dispatched the devil and undone the pact her father made to give her away, the family may enjoy the trunks of riches the demon has piled up in the house. They are set for life, one would think, but the maiden with no hands has other plans. "I want to go away from here," she tells her father. "Merciful people will give me all that I need to survive." As she prepares for her departure, the girl asks to have her two chopped-off hands tied onto her back. Then, at sunrise she sets out, walking and walking the entire day until nightfall. The journey takes her to a king's garden near a castle. Seeing an apple tree there, she suddenly grows hungry and, having no hands to pick the apples, she "shakes the tree with her body." When the apples fall to the ground, the maiden must pick them up with her teeth to eat them.

Seeing the thief, the night watchman apprehends her and turns her over to the king. The king orders her imprisonment, but his son, the prince, takes pity on the maiden and beseeches his father to release her. She can be a useful servant to them, he argues, and watch the hens in the courtyard. Of course, the prince falls in love with the unusual girl with no hands, and when it comes time for him to marry, he chooses her as his bride. Soon after the wedding, the young husband, now the king, is called to war and must depart, leaving his young—and pregnant—wife behind. When the baby is born, a series of messages that the king and queen send to one another by courier are tampered with by the same devil who had once stalked our heroine.

Altering the correspondence that the queen has sent her husband, the devil manages to deceive the king into believing that his newborn son is actually a changeling. The king is crestfallen with the news, but he still shows mercy for his young wife and does not wish to have her punished harshly. He sends this message home, but another fake letter written by the devil misinforms the court that the queen and her baby must leave the kingdom forthwith. Believing she must go into exile, the maiden with no hands is typically humble and stoic. She renounces her title as queen, saying "I have no good fortune, and I require none. Bind my child and my hands to my back. I will go out into the world."

Alone in the forest again, that place of symbolic transformation, our heroine happens upon a cottage. Sitting in front is an old man. "Please be so merciful," she begs him, "and hold my child to my breast so that I may nurse him." The kind man assists her. When the infant has finished nursing, he points to a large tree and directs the young woman to go to it and throw her stump arms around its trunk three times. Miracle of miracles, when she completes this ritual, her hands grow back entirely.

Divine intervention has made her whole again, and, in no time at all, the maiden and her baby are reunited with the king.

❧

In addition to the tremendous store of fairy tales the Hassenpflugs submitted to Jacob and Wilhelm, the sisters brought an unforeseen element to the collecting that posed a direct challenge to the brothers' notion that the narratives being transcribed were the quintessential expression of the collective German soul. The Hassenpflugs were Huguenots, and thus their home life was deeply influenced by French customs. For example, although the family had lived in Hesse for generations since the late 1660s, French was still spoken in their home, particularly at mealtimes. This family ritual was encouraged by the girls' mother, Marie Magdalene Hassenpflug, who had descended from a long line of Huguenots who had fled their native France in the late seventeenth century to escape the terrible anti-Protestant edicts passed by Louis XIV. Marie Magdalene's father, Étienne Droume, had been a minister, making him a prime target of the formidable royal proclamations demanding that anyone remotely recognizable as a Protestant be imprisoned or enslaved. Tens of thousands of Huguenots fled the Catholic country to practice their faith peaceably in neighboring Protestant lands. Droume settled his family in Hanau, which became one of the most important Huguenot centers for refugees to Germany. There Marie Magdalene grew up and raised her eldest daughters before the family moved to Kassel.

It was likely Marie Magdalene and her female servants told the young Hassenpflug girls the very tales that they would in turn pass along to Jacob and Wilhelm for their growing collection. Their stories, published in the first volume of the *Children's and Household Fairy Tales,* had descended directly from the seventeenth-century French fairy tale tradition, and particularly from the stories of Charles Perrault, the compiler and editor of the *Histoires ou Contes du Temps Passé* (Stories or Fairy Tales from Bygone Eras), also known as the legendary Mother Goose tales. Perrault's anthology was published in 1697, around the time of the great exodus of Huguenots from France who, as the Hassenpflugs' ancestors did, likely carried the stories with them to Germany. Though the Grimms and Hassenpflugs both shared deep connections to Hesse by dint of their association with Hanau and Kassel, this rich new source of stories was certainly not quintessentially Hessian, nor even German for that matter. In fact, tales such as "Red Riding Hood" and "Sleeping Beauty" were pan-European phenomena, predating even Perrault, with provenances tracing as far back as the Middle Ages and Ancient Greece. Nevertheless, Perrault's influence on the transmission of fairy tales to many parts of the Continent was tremendous, and the Hassenpflugs' involvement with the brothers Grimm played no small role in this literary wonder.

Charles Perrault's stories were not original creations, but collected oral material edited and fashioned by him into print. Interestingly, as with the Grimms, female storytellers were Perrault's main sources. He took what women had to tell, and then infused the stories with a cheeky style, maintaining a simple language meant to reflect the lives and wisdom of common folk. Often, he appended a moralizing conclusion to instruct boys and girls in proper behavior. His editorial process was uncannily similar to that of the brothers Grimm: No female source was ever cited by name.

In a working copy of the first volume of the *Children's and Household Fairy Tales*, Wilhelm penned the note "Marie 10 March 1811" in the margin of "The Maiden with No Hands."[5] These handwritten editorial notes that Jacob and Wilhelm made to themselves are the only systematic source, aside from scattered mentions in the brothers' correspondence, that tell us who the individual female contributors of each story were. Yet, in spite of this careful tracking of sources, the Grimms never credited their female collaborators by name in the formal publication of the tales. Instead, they described the Hassenpflugs' stories geographically in their foreword as stemming from "the region of the Main [River]." Similarly Friederike Mannels' tales were noted as coming from "the region of the Schwalm," the Wilds' simply from "Hesse."[6]

Thus, both Perrault's and the Grimms' fairy tale anthologies depended upon female storytellers for their greater dissemination throughout Europe, and indeed the world. As scholars, they placed their own names on the books they edited, but they allowed the identities of their collaborators to be subsumed by the idea that the stories represented not the ladies themselves but a far greater folk spirit, much in the way that the all-powerful patriarch in a fairy tale can demand sacrifices of his daughter in the name of a greater good.

"Bluebeard,"[7] contributed by Marie Hassenpflug, is a story with a long tradition in European folklore, and similar to "The Maiden with No Hands," for its heroine is betrayed by her own father, then subsequently stalked by an evil male antagonist. The story tells of a poor father who believes that a wealthy man who happens by his home one day can offer his daughter a better life. The mysterious suitor has a blue beard, which the girl finds eerily frightening. Under pressure from her father, she agrees to marry the strange man, but his bizarre beard keeps the girl on her guard. Once they are wed, Bluebeard tests his young bride's obedience. He gives her the keys to all the doors of his home before setting out on a journey, but she is forbidden, of course, to open one specific door. The naughty girl cannot contain her curiosity. The moment she sticks the key in the lock, the door flings wide open and "a flood of blood," we read, flows out at her feet.

Much to her horror, the girl beholds "dead females hanging on the walls of the forbidden room." Some of them, the story tells us, "were only skeletons." Our heroine is so terrified that she drops the key into the bloody pool at her feet. When she retrieves it, she finds that the blood has indelibly stained it. When Bluebeard returns home, he sees this telltale sign of his virgin bride's disobedience. In punishment, he begins to whet his knife, preparing to add her to his victims hanging on the wall. The girl screams for help, and coincidentally, her own brothers, who happen to be drinking wine and loitering in a nearby forest, hear her cries and rush to their sister's rescue in the nick of time.

The stalked woman is a standard motif in fairy tales, and in many respects, the message it imparted wove its way—albeit unconsciously—through the very method of collaboration that the brothers Grimm were engaged in as they adapted women's storytelling for publications that would bear their names. If the tales contributed by the women collaborators were noted only by the geographical region from where they came, then the deep underlying message of male literary culture was that women as individuals did not matter. Indeed, it was as if the ladies of the Hassenpflug and Wild households had no hands. Although they could read and write, they were nonetheless robbed of holding the symbolic quill of authorship.

THE SINGING BONE

"Just think," Dortchen Wild wrote to her friend Lotte Grimm while on a family trip away from Kassel, "I was at a big baptism last week. There were many people there, and naturally I had to offer my *hand* many times, but I would not remove my gloves at all!" It was the autumn of 1808, and Dortchen was only thirteen years old at the time, still shy of the feminine custom of offering one's hand to a young gentleman in greeting. Shaking hands made her positively squeamish, but, thankfully, that evening at a festive dinner following the baptism, she reported to Lotte, she had been seated between two old gentlemen, a far less difficult challenge than conversing with a young suitor. Besides, there were more important things to think of at the party, such as the "great deal" of food that was being served. "It tasted good," Dortchen raved, "which was my favorite thing about the whole affair."[1]

Ever since Dorothea Grimm's death, whenever Dortchen went away with her family, she worried like a mother hen about Lotte's gray disposition, and she was careful to write spirited letters home in an effort to cheer her friend. "Unfortunately," Dortchen joked about another social *faux pas* she had made while attending the baptismal party, "I had forgotten to bring my sewing bag to the table and had nothing with me except my knitting needles, one completed sock, and my handkerchief." Then she told Lotte how she had successfully stolen an extra piece of cake by hiding it inside the knitted sock, which she suddenly found to be a great convenience. How anyone didn't notice the tasty treat bulging inside the sock as she left the party was a wonder to her.[2]

In her correspondence, Dortchen's tone with Lotte was always confidential and sisterly, particularly when she got down to more confessional matters. "Dear Lottchen," she continued in the same letter, adding the diminutive *-chen* to her friend's name, "I would love it extraordinarily if you wouldn't show anyone my letters, for I would surely never write to you again, if I knew you had. The *thought* of your brother Wilhelm offering me his hand is far more to my liking than if he were to do it *in natura.*"[3]

A great deal had changed over the two years that had passed since Dortchen confessed this girlish crush on Wilhelm in her letter to Lotte. By 1810 she was fifteen, and it was no great secret that her fondness for her best friend's brother had matured into a more *mutual* attachment. Dortchen was beginning to catch

Wilhelm's attention in a manner far different from that of the early days when the Grimm family first arrived in Kassel. After returning from his long journey to Halle and Berlin, Wilhelm was keenly taken with this girl next door who had suddenly blossomed into a young woman. He greatly admired Dortchen now, and especially for her selfless devotion to her parents and for her open generosity toward his own parentless family. The tender feelings he harbored had transcended those playful games he used to entertain Dortchen with when she was a little girl. Wilhelm was twenty-four years old, and something solemn and bittersweet tugged at his heart whenever he had the opportunity of seeing Dortchen, who was ever the spirited and happy one among the guests at the weekly reading circle.

Every member of the Grimm family had felt a kinship with Dortchen from early on. Dorothea Grimm, before her death, had wished to have the endearing girl for a daughter; and Jacob included her in his personal family writings, a little book he had printed in 1810 to mark and preserve what was left of the Grimms' depleted lineage. "Forgive me, I have included you, sincere Dortchen," he wrote in the booklet, and confessed that he had done so to make the modest publication "more impressive" by her presence there. After all, he added, "all our relatives have nearly died off," and "I love you as I do my siblings, which certainly says enough."[4]

Though Jacob felt uninhibited in expressing his brotherly affections for Dortchen Wild in his memorial album, how and when she and Wilhelm finally confessed their love to one another is unknown. However, the following year, an unhappy event in the Grimm home made it clear beyond a doubt that Dortchen belonged to Wilhelm. On January 22, 1811, Jacob wrote a sorrow-ful letter to his friend Arnim saying that since Christmas the Grimms had "been living in a fear and anguish" that he could not "put down on paper" and indeed would never discuss. The problem had to do with Jacob and Wilhelm's wayward brother Ferdinand whom Jacob confessed he was much too fond of. In his eyes, Ferdinand was "far too good and obedient, better than the rest" of the siblings.[5] Jacob ended the baffling letter by beg-ging Arnim never to ask him what had happened. Then, two months later, mention of the mysterious crisis with Ferdinand surfaced once more, though all Jacob could say was that the situ-ation was "just as hopeless and helpless . . . as it was in the be-ginning." Jacob was ashamed. "It's something I don't want to write about," he repeated, adding that even though he was greatly attached to his research, "I would not think twice about giving it all up forever, if it could help matters. Indeed, God alone knows what the outcome will be."[6]

Though the Hassenpflugs' recent participation in the fairy tale anthology had been encouraging, the problem with Ferdi-nand was seriously impeding Jacob, who was obsessive when it came to his precious research and work routines. Something unspeakable had happened, something that could not be ut-tered aloud in fine company, and, whatever it was, it had sent Wilhelm's fragile health into another frightening downward spiral; indeed, the terrifying symptoms in his heart and breath-ing had returned with a vengeance.

What Arnim did not know was that Ferdinand Grimm had composed a story called "Aunt Henriette," the heroine of which was modeled on Dortchen Wild (her full Christian name being

Henriette Dorothea). In this fiction, Ferdinand portrayed himself as hopelessly in love with Dortchen, as much in love with her, in fact, as his brother Wilhelm was. Pained by the triangle, his only option was to kill his brother by poisoning him or shooting him. It's unclear whether Ferdinand ever made an attempt at taking Wilhelm's life, but his long-standing eccentricity and ill humor had suddenly taken on a dark force. He stayed up late into the night, often standing by the window whistling and staring into the darkness. The only living beings he seemed to love were his homing pigeons, which he tended to with great care, and he even built a special cage for them beside the house.

For years, Jacob and Wilhelm had seen this crisis coming. On one occasion, when Wilhelm was still in Halle under Doctor Reil's care, Jacob had written to his brother in a panic. "Each day things are getting more frightening with Ferdinand," he exclaimed. "If I were to ever wish that we were rich, it would be to know that he was independent."[7] Wilhelm shared Jacob's worries about their brother, who was musically gifted and a devoted reader, but he was more severe when stating his opinion about how to address Ferdinand's laziness and irritability.

Dortchen Wild, ever the friend and confidante to the Grimm family, had showed tolerance and even love for Ferdinand. He was often in her company while Wilhelm suffered through the long months of his medical treatments in Halle, and it was then, in a letter to Lotte, who was away in Marburg visiting Gretchen Wild, that Ferdinand confessed his passion. He had gone picnicking with Dortchen and another friend in the hills of Kassel, where they watched the grand fireworks that King Jerôme was putting on in another of his extravagant displays of power.

Spreading a blanket out on the grass for the girls, Ferdinand wrote that he lay down with them at their feet. "Lotte," he described the magical evening to his sister, "I have never experienced so much joy in seeing fireworks." The two girls liked them, too, and Dortchen especially liked the rockets as they soared up into the night sky. There were so many bright lights, he wrote, "that you could even see the person sitting right beside you, as if it were broad daylight," and if you could see a person in broad daylight, he concluded, then there was really no need to watch the fireworks: There was actually something "more beautiful" to see, Ferdinand confessed.[8] Dortchen Wild, her beauty illuminated by the bright rockets, was mesmerizing.

Whatever stability Reil's treatments might have provided to Wilhelm's poor heart, the mysterious incident of 1811 that Jacob could not bear to utter a word about even to his closest friend, Arnim, had sent Wilhelm into a depression. He soon stopped working altogether and spent a lot of time in bed. "You have no idea, dear Jacob, what sad moments, yes, sad hours that I'm experiencing," he wrote in an anguished letter to his brother, believing they were his last words before dying. "I'm rarely able to sit with all of you at the table without it so painfully and excruciatingly piercing my heart like an arrow. It's Ferdinand who causes this. He is living in a deep abyss. They say that where love is sown, joy will blossom, but nothing has blossomed inside him except a terrible self-affliction that knows of no God and is consoled by no heaven."[9]

At about this same time, Dortchen Wild had begun contributing fairy tales to the brothers' anthology with a sudden zeal and dedication. As the Hassenpflug sisters helped speed the pace of collecting with their new infusion of stories, Dortchen was becoming the project's most intimate source. Among the titles she added were "Hansel and Gretel" and "The Six Swans," and Wilhelm was always there to write them down, often meeting Dortchen in secluded romantic locations.

One of the stories Dortchen told Wilhelm during this period bizarrely mirrored the triangle that had erupted between her and the brothers Grimm. On a winter's day beside the oven in the greenhouse, Dortchen sat with Wilhelm and shared with him the tale of "The Singing Bone,"[10] a story about hateful rivalry between brothers who are competing for the same bride. "A wild boar was doing great harm throughout the land," Dortchen opened the story, as Wilhelm took down her words. "No one dared go into the forest where it ran around loose, and whoever was so bold as to attack it, wanting to kill it, [the boar] tore at his body with its tusks." Wanting to restore safety to the region, the king of the land proclaims that he will give his daughter in marriage to whoever kills the boar. Three brothers decide to try their luck at winning the princess, the two eldest banding together against the youngest. This constellation of older brother(s) versus younger was a typical plotline in the Grimm tales, and reminiscent of the eccentric Ferdinand, the youngest was always forced to go his way all alone. Wilhelm listened to Dortchen, this young woman he was falling in love with, tell the story of "The Singing Bone" with such gentle yet courageous insight into his complicated family life that it made his blood race.

When the youngest brother of the tale enters the forest in search of the wild boar, he encounters a little man who is holding a black lance in his hand. "Take this lance," the man tells him, "and hack away at the boar. Do it without fear. You will easily kill him." As was predicted by the strange man, our hero effortlessly slaughters the boar; then, swinging the dead animal onto his shoulder, he heads home, very satisfied in the knowledge that *he* is to marry the princess. Along the way, he passes by a tavern and finds his two older brothers drinking wine and making merry. They ask their younger brother to join them for a while. After they've had their fun, the three strike out for home together, but the happy familial scene isn't what it appears to be. Just as they're crossing over a bridge, the two eldest brothers grab the youngest one and beat him to death. Then, to cover up their terrible crime, they bury him underneath the bridge.

Some years later, a shepherd boy crosses the same bridge and spies a bone sticking out from the sand below, in the spot where the murdered man was buried. Thinking the bone will make a good mouthpiece for his horn, the boy pulls it out of the sand and begins whittling at it. When he puts it to his mouth to test it, the bone magically begins to sing:

> Ach, little shepherd boy,
> you're blowing on my tiny bone.
> My brothers are the ones who killed me
> and buried me beneath the bridge,
> so they could trade the wild boar
> for the king's young daughter.

Puzzled, the shepherd decides to show the king the amazing bone that tells riddles; but the king immediately understands the bone's message and sentences the two murderous brothers to death by drowning. Justice is served, and the story closes with the skeleton of the youngest brother exhumed and buried again in the proper place, his "lovely grave inside the churchyard." The power of the fairy tale to express core human emotions such as guilt, hatred, greed, and anger swirled about Wilhelm as he allowed Dortchen to touch with her story the wounded places in his own sad relationship with Ferdinand.

By the summer of 1812, Ferdinand gave up on their home in Kassel and decided to move to Munich to live with the youngest brother, Ludwig. At first, his departure was like a death in the family, and it tormented Jacob and Wilhelm with feelings of loss and failure. Even Ferdinand's pigeons refused to eat any longer, and the brothers found themselves forced to sell the birds off, "the most beautiful" of them, Jacob lamented in a letter to Arnim, fetching "only a penny." In spite of the sadness, however, it was as if "a stone [had] been lifted from our hearts," Jacob told Arnim. "We hadn't been—I don't know for how long—able to eat at the table in joyful demeanor."[11]

The whole affair left a rift between the brothers that, like the dark moral of a fairy tale, cursed them for many years. In 1814, Wilhelm wrote to Arnim about his thoughts on the matter: "I possess the kind of anger and pity for [Ferdinand] that I have for the foolish virgins in the Bible. He misses the boat—and complains about it afterward."[12] The story of "The Singing Bone" teaches that brotherly strife leads to irreparable damage and injustice in the family, and, like the characters in the very tales they were editing, the brothers Grimm were not invulnerable to the truths about human nature that the stories unforgivingly expressed.

Ferdinand's departure from Kassel had occurred during the most extreme economic crisis Europe had known since Napoleon had crowned himself emperor. France's escalating war budget and its army's bloated bureaucracy had depleted every resource—money, food, and manpower—across the entire European continent. Ever since the brothers had launched the fairy tale project in 1807, Bonaparte's demands for new recruits to the Grand Army had escalated to such a point that no country could realistically satisfy them. In Westphalia alone, the numbers of infantry battalions, cavalry squadrons, and artillery batteries soared during the very years that the Wilds and Hassenpflugs were busily gathering stories, and by 1811, Jerôme Bonaparte's kingdom was facing bankruptcy and the loss of its most productive men. In November that year, as Dortchen Wild was contributing some of her most compelling tales to the collection, Westphalia was forced to pay the costs of 35,000 troops quartered there, causing the national debt to soar from 60 million francs to more than 200 million.[13]

Life trudged on, and with Ferdinand gone, the brothers found they could return to their research with renewed attention. The project of collecting tales picked up speed, more than it had known since Dorothea Grimm's death, for Dortchen Wild, always the abiding witness to the Grimm family's personal calamities, fostered a spirit of hope for the project that kept the brothers going. She was the quintessential *Pflegerin*, or domestic worker. When all her sisters had married and moved away with their own families into their own homes, Dortchen remained with her parents; she tended to their feeble health, watched over the apothecary, oversaw the domestic chores, and forewent the prospect of marriage until her parents' deaths, many years later. When her sister Gretchen died prematurely, leaving four young children, Dortchen stepped in to raise the orphans as if they were her own.

One of the most precious stories Dortchen contributed to the *Children's and Household Fairy Tales,* "Frau Holle,"[14] featured a heroine much like herself, a girl of self-sacrificing perseverance and loyal service to her elders. In Germany today, "Frau Holle" is a classic that enjoys fame on the level of "Sleeping Beauty" and "Cinderella," though it is less known in other cultures. Just about every living German knows the turn of phrase, "Frau Holle is shaking out her feather bed," which passes over lips at the first sign of snowfall; indeed, the snowflakes, floating gently down from the wintry sky, resemble stray feathers drifting out from a well-fluffed bed.

"A widow had two daughters. One was beautiful and dutiful, the other ugly and lazy," the story begins. The mother, we learn, spoils the indolent and disrespectful girl, who lives a life of ease while her lovely, conscientious sister must do all the housework. One day, the beautiful sister goes out to fetch water from the well. As she's bending over the edge to pull the heavy bucket up, she falls inside. When she awakens, she finds herself sitting in a lovely sunny meadow surrounded by "many thousands of flowers." Walking through the meadow, the girl happens upon an oven full of bread. The bread is enchanted and calls out to her: "Ach, take me out, take me out, otherwise I'll burn!" The faithful girl is quick to respond, pulls the bread out, and then continues on her way. Soon, she arrives at a tree laden with apples. "Ach! Shake me! Shake me!" the tree calls to her. Then the apples chime in, "We apples are ripe!" The girl obeys and shakes the tree, bringing all the ripe apples down before she continues on her way. Finally, she comes upon a little house. An old woman sitting inside looks out at her through the window. The girl is afraid and wants to run away because the woman has big teeth. "Fear not, dear child," the old woman calls out to her. "Stay with me. If you do all the housework in my home, and if you are tidy about it, then you will do well. But you must pay special attention making my bed, and shake it out diligently so that the feathers drift around. That's how it snows in the world. I am Frau Holle."

The girl trusts the woman's kind words and works in her service. Upon seeing that the maiden's labors are very satisfactory, especially the way she shakes the feather bed out with great heft, Frau Holle offers her apprentice "a good life," the story tells us. In exchange for her work, no ill word is spoken against the girl, and every day she is allowed to eat "something boiled and something roasted." The truth that a woman's domestic abilities were one of her only means of securing a decent living was relevant even to a young middle-class girl such as Dortchen Wild. Earning one's keep, and with luck, earning it in wedlock in a home of her own, was the most she might hope for in life, particularly with the great war raging and killing off hundreds of thousands of marriageable men.

After living with Frau Holle for some time, our heroine becomes homesick. The old woman is merciful and grants the girl leave because she has "served so faithfully." Leading her apprentice from the house, Frau Holle brings her to an enormous gate. As the girl approaches, the gate opens magically all by itself. When she crosses its threshold, a "powerful golden rain" begins to fall upon her, covering her body in riches. "This is for you because you have been so diligent," Frau Holle explains. The maiden bids the old woman farewell and exits the gate, whereupon, the story tells us, she is restored again to "the world."

Our heroine returns home and, when her mother sees her daughter bedecked in gold, she naturally takes the girl back in. When she hears her daughter's story of Frau Holle and her amazing kingdom, the greedy woman decides to send her favorite daughter, the ugly, lazy girl, to garner even more riches. The bad girl intentionally throws herself down the same well that her sister had fallen into. Then she, too, wanders through the same meadow and is tested by the same oven and the same apple tree. But the lazy maiden refuses to serve these enchanted objects; she does not save the bread from burning, nor does she release the ripe apples. When she reaches Frau Holle's cottage, she has no fear for the old woman's big teeth. She knows that they are harmless. On the first day of her service, the girl truly makes an effort, following Frau Holle's every order. But she does everything with only the gold in mind. By the second day, the maiden begins to show her true colors and shirks the chores she is told to perform. By the third day, she has completely returned to her old bad habits, not even wanting to get out of bed in the morning. Worst of all, she doesn't shake out Frau Holle's bed with enough force to throw the feathers up in the air. This annoys the old woman, and she fires the girl. But the girl is happy with the decision, for she assumes that when she leaves the kingdom, the same golden rain that fell upon her sister will also pour riches over her. But as the defiant maiden passes through the threshold of the magical gate, a "giant kettle full of pitch" spills on her and oozes over her body. "That is your reward for your services," Frau Holle scolds the indolent girl. Such transgressions, the story teaches, are indelible, for when the wretched girl arrives home, she is unable to remove the dark pitch from her body for the rest of her life, a symbol of her domestic failure.

The bad sister of "Frau Holle" was certainly not a candidate for marriage, though her good sister, who fit the mold of the conscientious caregiver and house cleaner, would certainly achieve this goal. Wilhelm Grimm witnessed Dortchen's sacrifice for her family with respect and admiration. Her ability to keep her equilibrium in the face of extreme hardship resonated deeply with the Grimms' own familial values. One day, Wilhelm was beginning to feel, he just might marry this special girl from next door.

8

A CHRISTMAS BOOK

Just a few days after Dortchen Wild told Wilhelm
Grimm the story of "The Singing Bone," Achim von Arnim
turned up in Kassel on a surprise visit. His wife, Bettina, was
traveling with him and was pregnant with their first child. The
young couple had been on a long honeymoon and, making their
way back home, stopped in Kassel for a few days to see the
Grimms, as well as Bettina's sister and brother-in-law, who also
lived in the city. "He was with us for an entire day," Wilhelm
shared with Aunt Zimmer the details of their friend's visit.[1] The
brothers had presented Arnim with all their meticulously kept
transcriptions of the stories, which the poet pored over in
amazement. Bettina could not join her husband on his trips to

the Grimm home, for it was much too burdensome, particularly in the dead of winter, for a woman with child to make the walk, or even a carriage ride, all the way to the Marktgasse.[2] Instead, the Brothers made a point of visiting Bettina every afternoon for tea at her sister's house. They had always had a staunch supporter of the fairy tales in Arnim, but they now were discovering that his soulful young wife (who was also Clemens Brentano's sister) shared as much enthusiasm and penetrating literary insight for the collection as her husband.

Bettina was born in Frankfurt in 1785, the same year as Jacob. She was so fond of the brothers that she, together with her husband and her brother, Clemens, became a benefactor of young Ludwig Grimm, supporting him as he made his way through art school. Like her brother Clemens, Bettina had always felt at home in artistic and literary circles. By the time she was in her early twenties, she had developed an intimate relationship with Goethe's mother and eventually she met Goethe himself. She visited the renowned author for the first time in 1807, when she was an aspiring writer of only twenty-two. From that visit, she maintained a correspondence with her literary idol, journeying to see him several more times in Weimar before his death in 1832.

On the auspicious occasion of the Arnims' visit to Kassel in January 1812, Bettina expressed her high regard for the breadth and content of the brothers' growing anthology, which bolstered their confidence to press forward with publication. Her husband Achim was so astonished by Jacob and Wilhelm's achievement that he wrote immediately to Brentano, ignoring what his brother-in-law might think about the competition. "In Kassel for several days with the Grimms," he dashed out the letter, "very satisfied among books and manuscripts." The brothers, Arnim reported, had not only become "even more sharp-witted and erudite" but had also made "enormous progress with their collections."[3]

The Arnims urged Jacob and Wilhelm to find a publisher without further delay, convincing them that a project of such magnitude—the brothers had originally set out to collect *every* story ever told in the German language—would never reach perfection. Arnim even offered to present the manuscript to his own publisher, Reimer, in Berlin, regardless of his brother-in-law's plans for a book of stories.

In this moment, Jacob and Wilhelm were released from any obligation they felt to Brentano, and they accepted their friend's offer. By June, Arnim happily reported in a letter from Berlin that Reimer wanted to print the fairy tale collection. The publisher had even sketched out the terms of a contract, which would earn Jacob and Wilhelm a "certain honorarium" once a prescribed number of copies had been sold. It was a modest beginning, but given the woeful economic situation of Europe in 1812, it was very easy for Jacob and Wilhelm to accept the publisher's terms. "Reimer's offer regarding our fairy tale collection," Wilhelm wrote to Arnim, "is very agreeable to us." Because the production of the book would be compact and ordinary, he added, the publisher would in no way be risking too much. The brothers also pledged to send more stories: "As soon as we have a free hand, we want to expand the manuscript."[4]

Expand they did. With the Wild and Hassenpflug sisters at their disposal, the summer and autumn of 1812 brought further stories, and at a pace that would never be paralleled again in the history of collecting for the *Children's and Household Fairy Tales*. The quality of the stories—in large portion these were *the* Grimm classics, the ones known most widely throughout the world today—and their having been collected in person from the brothers' women friends fired the process with an unusual feeling of geniality and purpose.

"Red Riding Hood"[5] was one of the most significant stories to appear in volume one of the *Children's and Household Fairy Tales*. A gem of a tale contributed by Marie Hassenpflug, it would establish the Grimm name as a household term in countries all around the world. Transcribed in the autumn of 1812, during the brothers' rush to produce a solid manuscript for Reimer, the story Marie told to Jacob and Wilhelm had *two* parts, both of which had originally appeared in volume one of the *Children's and Household Fairy Tales;* though the more subversive second part is often expunged in modern editions of the stories. In the classic version of "Red Riding Hood," the heroine is a typical fairy tale victim. Though her mother tells her not to stray from the path on the way to her grandmother's house, the infamous wolf in the forest tricks her into picking a bouquet of flowers for her granny. When the girl wanders off the path in search of flowers, the wolf rushes ahead to the grandmother's house. There, he gobbles up the old lady, then, after donning the old woman's clothes and bonnet to disguise himself, he patiently waits for Red Riding Hood. When the unsuspecting girl arrives at the cottage, the wolf swallows her up, too. But a huntsman saves the day, arriving on the scene in the nick of time. Slitting open the wolf's belly, he rescues both ladies, who emerge from their persecutor's stomach safe and uninjured. The story ends with a moral directed specifically at girls who won't obey their mothers: "Never again in your life," Red Riding Hood scolds herself, "will you wander off the path in the forest when mother has forbidden it."

In this commonly known version of "Red Riding Hood," the female victim, rather than her attacker, is implicitly blamed for the violence she suffers; but in Marie Hassenpflug's second telling of "Red Riding Hood," grandmother and granddaughter come off in a much different light. In this now obscure and relatively unknown version, Red Riding Hood visits her old grandmother a second time and brings the gift of a cake. As she is on her way to the cottage, another wolf tries to deceive the girl, asking her what she has hiding beneath her little smock. It is the cake, naturally, but the dialogue is sexually charged in its ambiguous reference to what could be hiding beneath that little dress. Red Riding Hood, the clever maid, won't be seduced this time and sticks to the straight and narrow path. When she arrives at her grandmother's house, she tells her granny that she has seen a wolf in the forest. He bid her good day, she says, but his eyes had gazed upon her so nastily that if "it hadn't happened on the open street, he would have eaten me."

"Come," her grandmother replies, "let's lock the door so that he can't get in." Of course, minutes later, the wolf comes knocking at the door and calls out, "Open up, grandma. I'm Red Riding Hood. I'm here to bring you a cake." But the women are still as mice. Foiled by their cleverness, the wolf must take a new tack. Circling the house several times in consternation, he finally decides to jump onto the roof. There he will wait, he thinks to himself, until Red Riding Hood leaves for home that evening. He will then sneak after her in the dark and eat her. But grandma is much too wise in this version of the tale. "I cooked some sausages yesterday," she tells her granddaughter, and directs the girl to fetch the bucket and carry the cooking water to the stone trough that's just outside the door of the house. The girl obeys her granny and carries buckets full of sausage water until the big trough is filled. The smell of the sausages wafts up to the roof where the wolf is waiting. He sniffs and sniffs. Then, seeing the water down below in the trough, he leans over the edge of the roof, stretching his neck so far that he loses his grip, plunges down into the water, and drowns. The story ends on a happy note when Red Riding Hood is able to leave her grandmother and walk safely home.

Both parts of Marie Hassenpflug's telling of "Red Riding Hood" read like teachings on how to avoid being raped. The second part of the story, however, is far more affirming of women's strength and independence. Here we have no hero to save the ladies, nor the moralizing conclusion that blames the victim. But given the culture of the period and its devaluation of women's strength and intellect, it's no wonder that a self-sufficient girl and her intelligent grandma couldn't survive their relegation to obscurity, much in the way that we know so little of the women who told the stories.

While the Hassenpflugs put in their share of tales, more were streaming in from the Wild household, too, amounting to nearly thirty titles by the time of publication. Some of Gretchen's nearly thirty titles by the time of publication. Some of Gretchen's submissions included a version of "Child of Mary"; "The Companionship of Cat and Mouse," a domestic tale about two animals who set up house together; "Prince Swan," a story about a girl who saves a king from a spell that turned him into a swan; and "The White Dove," the tale of a simpleton who breaks a magic curse that has kept a princess in the form of a dove. Mie Wild added "Godfather Death," the story of a poor man who, while looking for someone to be the godparent of his thirteenth born, accepts Death's offer to represent the child. Dortchen Wild's additions tallied up to an astounding repertoire, among them "Frau Holle," "The Singing Bone," "Rumplstiltskin," and versions of "Fitcher's Bird" and "King Thrushbeard." She also contributed "Princess Mouseskin," a story about a wise princess who is disowned by her father. So that she can make her way in the world, the girl has a special skin fashioned from the fur of a mouse. When she wears it, she is able to transform her identity. Another story of Dortchen's, "All Fur," is similarly about a girl who wears a special pelt, made of the skins of every animal in the forest, to protect herself after nearly falling victim to her father's incestuous desire. Even Dorothea Katarina Wild, the girls' mother, had stories to share with Jacob and Wilhelm, including tales involving enchanted objects and speaking animals such as "The Travels of the Straw, the Cinder and the Bean" and "The Mouse and the Flea."

By September 1812, the brothers Grimm had collected dozens of new fairy tales since their decision to publish. "We've been outright diligent this summer," Jacob wrote to Arnim in a

Berlin. "Since you were last here, our collection has enriched it-self a great deal," he gushed with pride, and emphasized that be-cause all the newly added tales had been transcribed from direct storytelling, the book would be "rich and charming." The broth-ers' process of collaboration with their women friends had caused Jacob to see "more clearly how significantly these old fairy tales [had] insinuated their way into the entire history of poesy."[6] That same year, Jacob and Wilhelm had managed to publish two other books pertaining to the history of German literature, both of them forgotten epics from the medieval era written in Old and Middle High German, the *Hildebrandslied* (The Song of Hildebrand) and the *Wessobrunnergebet* (The Prayer of Wesso-brunn). Like the fairy tales, these narrations were once shared as live performances, not by female storytellers but rather by court bards.

With the manuscript being typeset and readied for printing, the brothers' methodological separation from Brentano was now complete. Jacob wrote freely of the matter to Arnim, as if a tremendous burden had been lifted from him. "That Clemens' reworking [of the fairy tales] does not satisfy you makes me happy," he said. "I only regret the assiduousness and intellect he devoted to it. He can manipulate and embellish all he wants, but our simple, faithfully collected stories will surely always put his to shame."[7] Jacob was reiterating his belief that precise tran-scription of a storyteller's words was the most genuine method of capturing the spirit of bygone eras.

"The Magic Table, the Golden Donkey, and the Club in the Sack"[8] was a good example of a story that matched the brothers' ideal of faithful collecting. They had recorded two oral versions of the story, as told by Dortchen Wild and Jeanette Hassenpflug (who had reportedly heard it from an old Madame Storch). This story is a *Schwankmärchen*, or a tale of comical exploits typically experienced by a male protagonist. It opens with a hapless shoe-maker who is so poor that he must kick his three sons out of the house. The eldest boy decides to go into apprenticeship with a carpenter. He works for the man for one year, and when his training is completed, he prepares to go out into the big world to seek his fortune. Before his departure, the carpenter gives the young man a small table as a parting gift. Though quite ordinary in appearance, the object is enchanted, and whenever its owner says the magic words aloud, "Little table, set thyself," the table is miraculously covered with "a fine white table cloth, a golden plate, a golden fork, a golden knife, and a glass made of crystal that is filled with red wine." Then an array of tasty dishes appear as well. Taking the useful treasure with him, the young carpenter sets out on his way, and "no matter where he went," the story tells us, "in the field, in the forest, or in a tavern," whenever "he set his little table down and said 'Little table, set thyself' he had the most splendid meal" put before him.

One evening, the young man shows off in an inn, inviting everyone there to dine with him. The innkeeper, seeing the profit he can make from the endless supply of savory dishes, steals the enchanted table while his guest is asleep that night and replaces it with an ordinary one. The following morning, the young man returns home, wanting to please his penniless father by feeding the entire family. Everyone gathers round, thrilled about the forthcoming feast, but when the young man calls out the magic words, "Little table, set thyself," nothing happens. Disappointed, all the relatives go home "unwatered and unfed," and father and son must return to their toil once more.

The dream of living a life of plenty, without heavy labor, is strongly present in nearly every scene of this story. The shoemaker's second son also ventures out into the world and, after finishing an apprenticeship as a miller, receives a magical donkey named Brickelbrit as his parting gift. Whenever the donkey's name is uttered aloud—"Brickelbrit!"—the animal begins to "spew out coins, from the front and from the back," the story tells us. Of course, this brother ends up at the same inn and is robbed of his special prize by the same conniving innkeeper. He, too, returns home only to fail in the eyes of his father for not producing the gold coins he promises. His fate remains that of any poor wretch, the story teaches: In the end, he must feed himself by practicing his trade.

Now, the third and youngest brother also happens to be the smartest, a common feature in fairy tales about male siblings, no doubt satiric commentary on old legal customs regarding the male hierarchy of authority and inheritance in the family. This youngest brother becomes a wood-turner, but his reward, upon completing his apprenticeship, is neither food nor money; instead, it is a "club in a sack." Whenever the owner of this enchanted object utters these magic words, a club immediately jumps out of the bag and, prancing around, begins to beat mercilessly anyone who happens to be standing nearby. Because he is the wisest of the three sons, the wood-turner knows that his brothers were robbed of their prizes. So he goes directly to the infamous inn with his own devious plan to dupe the greedy innkeeper. He tells the man that his two older brothers mistakenly left their precious table and valuable donkey behind at the inn, adding that what he has with him inside the sack is "even more precious and valuable." Naturally, the innkeeper is curious and, "thinking that all good things come in threes," he cooks up a scheme to steal the third brother's treasure in the middle of the night. The wood-turner, however, places his sack beneath his pillow, so that when the innkeeper sneaks into his room and begins pulling at it, he is awakened. "Club out of the sack!" the wood-turner yells. Instantly, the violent club springs forth and dances with the innkeeper, then beats him "so ruthlessly that [the man] gladly promise[s] to hand over the table and the donkey, Brickelbrit." Happy with his victory, the youngest brother heads home, bringing all three magical objects to his father. The poor family is now rich, and they live in happiness and joy.

"The Magic Table, the Golden Donkey, and the Club in the Sack" was a popular fairy tale in Europe during the Napoleonic Wars because it leant itself so well to political metaphors of power, greed, and, most important, the hope for triumph harbored by many a poor commoner. Each enchanted object represented the lowest common denominators of human survival: food, money, and, lacking these necessities, violence to claim, or reclaim, one's due. The weak *can* defeat the powerful, the story optimistically teaches, particularly when the powerful become too sated and blind in their own greed. This was beginning to happen to Napoleon Bonaparte. The very month that

Jeanette Hassenpflug told "The Magic Table, the Golden Donkey, and the Club in the Sack" to the brothers for transcription, the Russian army had become something of a "club in the sack" for the French. The punishing Battle of Borodino, fought over the two fateful days of September 6 and 7, 1812, rocked Napoleon's confidence profoundly as the Russians gave his massive army an unanticipated fight for their money. But, like the greedy innkeeper in "The Magic Table, the Golden Donkey, and the Club in the Sack," the bait of Moscow only made Napoleon hungrier. In spite of his heavy losses at Borodino, the emperor advanced his sick and weakened troops deeper into Russia, but he ignored the signs of the approaching cruel winter. He also disregarded his own failing health. He was growing fat, he could no longer mount his horse without assistance, and he had lost the crystalline thinking for military strategy that he had relied upon so instinctively in his youth. Though the Grand Army managed to occupy Moscow, they were surprised to find the magnificent city abandoned by its citizens. The soldiers looted buildings and homes, then languished there for most of the autumn, the famous comet of 1812 hanging in the heavens above them like a bad omen. Soon supplies grew scarce. Winter set in, and it was clear that the French would have to move into a mammoth retreat if they were to find food. This is when Napoleon gave the fateful call to leave Moscow and misguidedly ordered his soldiers to double back on a trek through the battlefields of Borodino. The ill-conceived maneuver shook their confidence when they marched through the field where the bones of 30,000 rotting corpses were being picked clean by wolves and crows.[9]

The *Children's and Household Fairy Tales* was published in the same moment that news of the French retreat from Moscow and of Napoleon's cowardly abandonment of his own army was spreading through Europe like wildfire. England, Prussia, and Austria immediately began to forge new alliances in preparation for the ouster of the reviled Bonaparte family, including King Jerôme of Westphalia, from their thrones across the Continent. Perhaps a victory for the little man, the penniless family, the beleaguered widow, and the fatherless child—all stock characters of fairy tales who had their parallels in living German society—was just around the corner.

❧

Achim von Arnim was in Berlin when the first printing of the *Children's and Household Fairy Tales* rolled hot off the press, and he received copies of the volume from Reimer long before the brothers themselves saw the publication that had taken them five years to complete. After weeks of printing delays, more copies were finally sent to Kassel, on December 20, just in time for Christmas.

Christmas Eve of 1812 was a glorious day for Bettina von Arnim. She found a copy of the Grimms' *Children's and Household Fairy Tales* waiting for her as a present. She took the book— "bound in a handsome, hopeful green with gold trim," as she later described it—into her hands, opened it, and found to her amazement and delight that Jacob and Wilhelm had dedicated the volume to her and to her firstborn son, Johann Freimund. Reading her baby's name in print, Bettina later confessed, had "extracted a secret exultation from [her] breast."[10] Then, reading the foreword to the book, which was filled with metaphors Jacob and Wilhelm had chosen to describe the underappreciated fairy tales, Bettina must have felt that the brothers' words just as easily could have depicted all the women of Kassel who had played such a critical role in their collecting.

"We find it virtuous," the foreword went,

> when a storm or some other misfortune sent down from heaven beats down upon an entire field, striking it to the ground, so that only in the low hedges or bushes along the side of the road a small place of shelter results, where single ears [of corn] remain standing. If the sun shines favorably again, they continue to grow, alone and unnoticed. No sickle severs them for the large storage bins, but in late summer, when they have become ripe and full, poor, pious hands come in search of them. And ear upon ear, they are carefully bound and more highly esteemed than an entire bushel. They are carried home, and all winter long, they will be nourishment, or perhaps they [will be] the only seeds for the future.[11]

LITERARY PRIVILEGE

Volume one of the *Children's and Household Fairy Tales* was received with some criticism. For readers who felt the stories were published solely for a young audience, reactions were similar to those seen even today; the tales were too vulgar and violent for young minds, hardly appropriate for the nursery. Still more readers, in academic and educated circles, were astonished to find that such simpleminded fare had made its way into print. The Grimms themselves viewed the book as an opportunity to test the waters.

In some respects, Jacob and Wilhelm had hoped that the publication would attract even more submissions of fairy tales from collaborators across the German-speaking regions, which they would edit and integrate into subsequent volumes. But the brothers would not have had the confidence for quickly gathering enough material for a second volume of stories had they not encountered a new substantial source that strangely paralleled previous collecting patterns. The new family of storytelling daughters was the von Haxthausens. Wilhelm was the first to make the acquaintance of these aristocratic ladies, when he journeyed, in the summer of 1811, to Bökerhof, one of the von Haxthausens' rural estates located in central Germany near the small township of Brakel. Wilhelm had come to know the sisters' brother, Werner von Haxthausen, a scholar of old Greek folk songs, during his gloomy months in Halle under Dr. Reil's care. At the time, Werner had encouraged him to come to Bökerhof, where Wilhelm was certain to find a wealth of tales.

Hoping to enhance what the Hassenpflugs and Wilds had already given to volume one, Wilhelm made the trip in July. It was refreshing to leave Kassel again. Two years had passed since his last travels, and the rolling farmland and gentle forests of the landscape around Bökerhof were pleasing to the eye. On the way there, however, things took a sudden turn for the worse. Wilhelm described a leg of the trip in a letter to Jacob: "I rented a small wagon that cost only twenty pennies," he wrote. The cheap fare must have meant a rickety wagon, because twice it flipped over along the way. Not wanting to risk a third accident, Wilhelm made the rest of the journey on foot. It took several hours to walk the long distance, and it taxed his heart, but finally, he "arrived on Saturday at four," he told Jacob, and was received "very graciously."

Although Wilhelm was physically depleted, Werner von Haxthausen's "pleasant and delicate" sisters lifted his spirits immediately. That very evening, the young women gathered in the foyer of the house to sing folk songs. This was a home that prided itself on old German customs and simple living, albeit with a stylized romantic gentility. "It was very lovely, and I wished that you could have heard it, too," Wilhelm wrote of the ladies' songs. "You have no idea how marvelously tender all the melodies are."[1]

Werner was away, traveling on business, and with time his connection with Wilhelm waned, but his sisters' involvement in the fairy tale anthology more than made up for it. Four of the seven von Haxthausen daughters, aged from ten years to thirty-four, and a second brother named August, immediately showed a propensity for collecting folklore that seemed to be much attuned to the Grimms' methods and ideals regarding the concept of the *Volk*. The ladies, Wilhelm enthusiastically reported to Jacob, had copied the songs they sang onto small vellum papers, "creating their own delicate little anthology."[2]

One day during his stay at Bökerhof, Wilhelm asked the youngest of the sisters, ten-year-old Anna, to take a walk with him through the lovely linden tree arbor that gracefully circled the perimeter of a field outside the family's stately home. As he walked with the little girl beneath the cathedral of leaves that arched above them along the path, Wilhelm asked Anna to tell him a story. Whatever tale the girl related that auspicious day—there is no record of the title—remains a mystery, but it launched another important collaboration for Jacob and Wilhelm, garnering them seventy-five new stories.

Unlike the Hassenpflug and Wild sisters, who were of the middle class, the aristocratic von Haxthausens possessed more time and leisure to sustain such literary pursuits. Anna, Sophie, Ludowine, and Ferdinandine took particular interest in the project. For them, gathering stories was a natural extension of their family's already well-established love and knowledge of folklore.

Compared to the narrow rooms of the Grimms' apartment in Kassel, Bökerhof was spacious and graced. The lovely estate and the von Haxthausen name had an illustrious history in the region around Brakel that dated back to the fourteenth century, when the family ancestors received a fiefdom of several estates from the prince-bishop of Paderborn. In earlier eras, the von Haxthausen patriarchs had administered all church and legal affairs in the region, and by the middle of the eighteenth and early into the nineteenth centuries, the house at Bökerhof became the destination of the family's Romantic literati. This generation of fifteen children were the progeny of Baron Werner Adolf von Haxthausen. With his first wife, Luise von Westfalen zu Hedelbeck, the baron had fathered one daughter, who would later give birth to Annette von Droste-Hülshoff, arguably Germany's foremost female author and poet of the nineteenth century. The baron's second wife, Maria Anna von Wendt zu Papenhausen, gave birth to fourteen children, seven sons and seven daughters, the "pleasant and delicate" ladies Wilhelm had written home to Jacob about.

In the years of the Napoleonic Wars, it became a tradition for the writers and scholars of the von Haxthausen and the von Droste-Hülshoff branches of the family to gather at Bökerhof

for collaborative summers. Their folkloric activities soon at-
tracted the attention of other German intellectuals and artists
from across Europe, including the brothers Grimm. Even if it
was too late to include in volume one whatever tales the ladies
might gather, Wilhelm left Bökerhof knowing that he would
see them again, for he had discovered a vein of gold.

In January 1813, a few weeks after the publication of volume
one of the *Children's and Household Fairy Tales*, Wilhelm penned a
letter to Ludowine von Haxthausen, the eldest of the sisters,
and sent her a copy of the new book as a methodological cue
for collecting. "Allow me, madam," he wrote, "to renew my re-
membrance with you and your sisters through this small volume of fairy tales, which you, as I hope, will read with pleasure,
either because of the stories themselves, or because you remember the time when you once heard them with pleasure. This collection is very dear to my brother—who, not knowing you yet,
sends his best wishes—as well as to me. We would like to make
it as complete as possible, and therefore, I would like to take
the liberty of asking you for contributions: entirely new pieces
that we're still missing, or elaborations and corrections to the
old ones. Nothing is too insignificant for us. We will gladly
accept any trifle." Then, appealing to the ladies' deep folkloric
insight that he had witnessed in Bökerhof that previous summer, Wilhelm added that he did not doubt that his new collaborators could share some stories with him "in the singular,
lovely way in which folklore still live[d]" in their home. He
continued: "I am also certain that you are poised to do it in the
manner that I most prefer, and that is faithfully and precisely,

with every idiosyncrasy, even dialect, without additions and so-called beautification."[3]

One week later, a package arrived in Kassel. It contained a treasure trove of stories and folk songs that the von Haxthausens had been collecting assiduously for months. Wilhelm wrote in reply to the ladies' brother August, who had assisted in orchestrating the effort: "Dear H., I have just received your letter of January 21 with the rich enclosure of fairy tales and songs and with great joy," Wilhelm gushed with delight, adding that the manuscripts were "dear and correct" and that he had "no criticisms" of the manner in which August had transcribed the tales. "It is loyal and simple, just as I had desired it, and if you continue in this fashion, as you promised me, you will play no small part in the continuation of the book."[4] Although August took on the role of impresario in the collecting effort, it was really mainly his sisters who had gathered the tales for the manuscript that arrived at the Grimms' home in the mail.

One of the stories included in the package, "The Maiden of Brakel,"[5] was particularly pleasing to Jacob and Wilhelm, for it was submitted in a dialect spoken in the region around Paderborn. For the brothers, this was a mark of folk authenticity; indeed, the von Haxthausen sisters' ability to deliver precisely, in practice, what the Grimms had wanted in theory was pointing toward a far less painful collecting process than they had encountered while gathering sources for volume one. Ironically, it was these women of high education, privilege, and erudition in folkloric scholarship who could deliver with fidelity narratives of the simple life of commoners that the brothers had so passionately sought to publish.

One such story, "The Maiden of Brakel," was a cheeky narrative of feminine defiance, refreshing in comparison to the stories of victim-heroines so often encountered in fairy tales. "Once there was a maiden from Brakel who went to Saint Anne's Chapel at the foot of the Hinnenberg," the story opens, and includes some local lore of the region where the von Haxthausen family had its vast estates. Saint Anne was the patron saint of Brakel, and the Hinnenberg a mountain located very near Bökerhof. The maiden of the story has gone to the chapel to pray to Saint Anne for a husband, an appropriate pilgrimage for a girl, because Saint Anne is also the patron saint of housewives, mothers, and pregnant and childless women. In the gospels, she is the mother of the Virgin Mary. Thinking no one else is in the chapel, the maiden of Brakel sings her prayer aloud to Saint Anne:

> Holy Saint Anne,
> Please help me get my man.
> Oh, you know him, I'm sure.
> He lives down by the Suttmer Gate.
> His hair is yellow and quite pure.
> Oh, you know him, I'm sure.[6]

The town sexton happens to be standing behind the altar, where the maiden cannot see him. "You won't get him! You won't get him!" he harshly screams, mocking the girl's prayer. In doing so, he is deriding her sexuality, her desire for a husband and home, and, by extension, her only real shot at escaping poverty. The maiden thinks the voice she hears in the chapel is that of the Virgin Mary admonishing her. In church statuary and paintings, Saint Anne is typically depicted with her daughter, the mother of Christ, seated on her lap. The fairy tale assumes this knowledge in its listeners. It also assumes the listener will associate the Virgin Mary with the immaculate conception, or the idea that Mary gave birth without losing her virginity. The maiden of Brakel, looking at the image of Saint Anne and her child, saucily yells at the little Virgin sitting in her mother's lap, "*Tra-la-la,* you stupid brat! Hold your tongue, and let your mother speak." The story ends abruptly with that, and it certainly must have elicited rebellious peals of laughter from young women of the age who saw the dark humor of it. The maiden of Brakel will not be placed on lower moral ground for wanting her man and, by implication, for wanting sex. After the maiden gives the prudish Virgin a piece of her mind, we hear nothing more of the sexton. He stands silenced behind the altar.

As Jacob and Wilhelm refined their definition of the fairy tale genre, they began to see a plethora of new material they could collect in the way of old sayings, idioms, and local legends passed down generation to generation. "The Maiden of Brakel" was actually more a legend than it was a fairy tale because its themes were locally determined by the lore of a particular region or town. In fact, the Grimms' new association with the von Haxthausens prompted them to undertake a completely new anthology, later published under the title *Deutsche Sagen* (German legends), to which the sisters contributed just as generously as they had to the fairy tale anthology.

The von Haxthausens were productive and tenacious collaborators. To Jacob and Wilhelm's great surprise, the transcribed material sent to them only three months after the publication of volume one of the *Children's and Household Fairy Tales* contained enough stories for half a book. "Anna is a Child of Fortune," Ludowine wrote, praising her youngest sister's gift at collecting stories. "She fishes everything out before the rest of us can even get to it! It must have to do with her trusting air. It doesn't matter where she goes, people like to tell her stories more than they do us."[7] The sisters, it seemed, had effortlessly developed a rapport with the old maids and grandmothers of the neighboring towns of Bökendorf, the tiny village where the Bökerhof estate was located. Whenever they arrived somewhere in search of new stories, the townsfolk knew why the women had come and would call out to one another on the street, "The Misses of Bökendorf are coming!" What set these ladies apart from previous female contributors to the Grimm anthologies was their methodical approach in scouring the countryside for new sources and their knowing just how to start people talking. In this way, the von Haxthausen women collected stories from the very people who fit the Grimms' ideal of the *Volk:* illiterate shepherds, old village women, and nursemaids. The stories they added to the collection included "The Bremen Town Musicians," a classic story about a donkey, a dog, a cat, and a rooster who, abused by their human masters, band together to oust a gang of robbers from their den, whereupon they make it their new home.

Another significant tale was "Devil Greencoat"[8] (also known in later editions as "Bearskin"), a story with a long tradition in Europe. More than 180 variations of this tale have been traced on the Continent alone, though the Grimm anthology put it on the map as one of the most entertaining "devil stories" of all time. It is a tale of three brothers. The eldest two, as might be expected, always browbeat the youngest. When it's time for all three boys to leave home and go out into the world, the mean older brothers tell the youngest one, "We don't need you. You must rove around on your own." And so they abandon him. It is often the sad lot of the youngest male in fairy tales to be the outsider of the family. Yet the plot usually unfolds in such a way that the poor wretch finds his way to a path of moral self-improvement that is far higher than the evil path his selfish brothers take. Without fail, his journey is fraught with risk, adversity, and often deep humiliation.

After his brothers leave him, the first thing our hero does is sit down and cry in despair. That's when Devil Greencoat appears: He has a horse's foot, the story tells us, and he is wearing a remarkable green coat. "What's wrong? Why are you crying?" the devil asks the young man. "My brothers have disowned me," our hero complains. So the devil offers the pitiful lad his assistance. "Put on this green coat," he says. "It has pockets that are always filled with gold. You can reach inside whenever you like. But in return, I demand that you not bathe for seven years, that you don't comb your hair, and that you don't pray. If you die during those seven years, then you are mine, but if you remain alive, then you are free—and rich no less—for the rest of your life." The young man agrees to the pact. Putting on the devil's green coat, he sticks his hand inside the pocket and finds that it is indeed full of gold.

The first year goes well for the lad. With his endless supply of money, he can pay for anything he wants. But in the second year, his life is not as easy. By now, we learn, his hair "had grown so long that no one recognized him, and no one wanted to give him shelter because he looked so disgusting." The longer his hair grows, the worse his luck becomes; but everywhere the young man travels he gives to the poor so that they will pray for him. The prayers, we are told, keep our hero from dying and falling into the hands of the devil.

On one occasion, the young man ends up helping a desperate old man by paying off all his debts to a greedy innkeeper. The old man, it so happens, has three beautiful daughters. In return for the good deed, the poor man tells his benefactor that he may wed the daughter of his choice. Our hero is covered in filth and hair by now, but he agrees to visit the old man's home. When the eldest daughter catches wind of her father's plan to marry one of the girls off to the atrocious monster who "no longer had a human face and looked like a bear," she screams. The second daughter rejects him, too, swearing that she'd rather leave home and live in the wide world all alone than marry him.

This is an important crux of the story. Unlike male protagonists, a female character of a fairy tale sets out into the world not to seek her fortune but rather to accept isolation and poverty and to forego all hope of stability, which can be brokered only by marriage. The youngest daughter, however, is the wisest and most obedient. "Dear father," she says, "because you made a promise [and the young man] helped you in your despair, then I shall obey you." Filled with joy, our hero takes a ring from his finger and breaks it in two, giving his betrothed one half and saving the other for himself. "Now I must take leave of you," he tells her. "I will stay away for three years. Be true to me, and when I return, we will have our wedding. But if I don't return in three years, then you are free, for I shall be dead. Pray for me that God will grant me life."

Freedom and autonomy were entirely different states of being for men and women of earlier centuries, as "Devil Greencoat" shows us. A man makes a pact with the devil because he hopes for a prosperous outcome. A woman, though she, too, desires prosperity, makes her pact not with the devil but with her future mate. Women's economic position in a society that did not allow them property and wealth made marriage the sole prospect and hope for a relatively painless existence, unless, of course, a girl was fortunate enough to be born into a landed and moneyed household, as the von Haxthausen children were. The privileged lady's version of autonomy and freedom then began to look more like that of her contemporary male peers. To lead a life of scholarship, writing—and even collecting fairy tales—was more acceptable in society for women of the highest class.

While the hero of "Devil Greencoat" is away from his bride-to-be for three years, she must endure the mockery of her older sisters, who jibe her for wanting to marry such a filthy man. But the tale boasts of her virtues, and of how she keeps her silence. While she waits for her groom to return, she admonishes herself to obey her father, "no matter what happens." Meanwhile, our hero, with his infinite stash of gold, is buying up gifts left and right for his future wife, doing "nothing evil but only good" wherever he can and "giving to the poor so that they will pray for him."

At last, when the three years are up, the young man has his long-anticipated reckoning with the devil, who arrives on the scene "grumbling and poisonous," demanding to have his green coat back. The hero removes the enchanted jacket "with joy," so uncorrupted has he remained from the riches he has possessed. The devil must keep his end of the deal, too, so he grants the young man wealth and "freedom" forever.

After his release, the young man runs home, bathes, and primps himself. Then he dashes to the house of his bride. When her father answers the door, the old man doesn't recognize the well-groomed fellow standing there before him. The lad pulls out his half of the broken ring. Lo and behold, his piece fits perfectly with that of the youngest daughter's. "And when she saw that he was a handsome man," the story reads, "she was filled with joy and loved him dearly, and they celebrated the wedding together."

The two older sisters who had behaved so poorly were in for a harsher fate. They were so "mad," the story tells us, for having missed their chance at catching such a good husband that, on the day of the wedding, "one drowned herself and the other hanged herself." That night, the devil comes to the newlyweds' home, pounding and grumbling at their door. The groom opens up to find the demon standing there in his infamous green coat. "You see!" the devil boasts gleefully. "I have two souls now, in exchange for your one!" Happy endings, it seems, are reserved only for girls who obey father and never mock the chance at marriage.

Essentially, "Devil Greencoat" is a story of the policing of women's autonomy. Interestingly, the words *free* and *freedom* appear several times in the tale, always in association with a pact. For the hero, pursuing freedom is his duty, something that, as a male, he must preserve at all costs, even if it requires slipping into beastliness for a certain time. For the heroine girl, however, freedom is an ominous power she may not touch, for if she possesses it, she may never marry; and thus, she will suffer an even harsher fate: poverty, death, or the loss of her very soul to the devil.

In later editions of the *Children's and Household Fairy Tales*, Jacob and Wilhelm published a second version of "Devil Greencoat" that incorporated new elements into the story drawn from a tale adapted from the oral tradition in the seventeenth century. In this account, the constellation of three brothers is done away with entirely. Instead, we see a solitary hero whose ill luck is no longer based upon his outsider status as the youngest male of the family but rather by his perceived uselessness as a soldier returning home from service in the war. The brothers Grimm subtly idealized the figure of the soldier in this new version of the story, influenced as they were by the long war they had been living through for most of their twenties. As Napoleon's demise was looking ever more certain, a nationalism never felt before by Germans began to make its way even into the stories the Grimms were editing.

Freedom was on the minds of many Germans, and after Napoleon's punishing defeat at Moscow in the winter of 1812, all of Europe watched as the French army, pursued by the Russians, moved in a panicky retreat from east to west across the Continent. In March 1813, Prussia declared war on France and mustered an army of soldiers fueled by a new patriotism that was beginning to replace the old feudal way of blind submission to one's sovereign.[9]

Napoleon was ill-prepared for a major test of the Grand Army's staying power. Over several years, he had lost hundreds of thousands of troops, and had suffered particular damage to his cavalry. The training and recruitment of new soldiers was sorely undermined by the sheer lack of men and by rising skepticism at home in France about his leadership. The Grand Army consisted mainly of old men and boys who had been conscripted at much too young an age. None were prepared for a major battle. By the summer of 1813, Russia and Austria joined Prussia in alliance against the French. Napoleon, still stunned by his losses in Moscow, was suffering from such dark depression that he kept a vial of poison tied around his neck so that he would be prepared to take his own life, should he wish to forego the agony of defeat. In the meantime, he would not go down on his enemies' terms, and he resisted the Allies' demands for peace and the restoration of the territories he had usurped. The famous "Battle of the Nations," fought near the city of Leipzig on October 16–19, 1813, proved to be the catastrophe for Napoleon that the Allies were waiting for. The French army consisted of a slim 160,000 depleted and untrained soldiers; the Allies had mustered 320,000 men. Though the defeat was not total, it left Napoleon at a complete loss for more reserves. In the weeks that followed, he managed a few victories in the German territories, including a skirmish in Hanau, the birthplace of the brothers Grimm.

Meanwhile, Ludwig and Karl Grimm wanted to join the Hessian army and were eventually placed together in the same division, Ludwig a lieutenant in the Third Ground Defense Regiment, Karl a volunteer guardsman on horseback. Ferdinand had wished to sign on, too, but missed his opportunity because he had fallen ill during the recruitment period. Jacob and Wilhelm heaved a sigh of relief at this news because they knew their eccentric brother's emotional frailty would surely endanger his life on the battlefield. Werner and August von Haxthausen also joined the military effort against the French, and on December 11, 1813, Wilhelm reported in a letter to their sister Ludowine that a friend of his had seen her brothers "several times and in good health" in the northern regions near Hamburg. Werner had been wearing a handsome red uniform; August, a green one. "How pleased I am," Wilhelm also wrote, "that our hopes from the summer have been so magnificently fulfilled," likely a reference about the impending fall of the French. "How lovely it will be to meet again after a happy peace," he continued. "We haven't had the courage to look upward, keeping ourselves [gazing down upon] the earth, lodged in our own forgetting." But now, Wilhelm felt, Germans would soon be able to lift their heads high again and feel joy.[10]

❧

In spite of the swirl of military dangers that dotted the map of Europe, efforts for volume two of the fairy tale anthology moved forward. Wilhelm had taken on the editorial helm of the project when Jacob was called to Paris in diplomatic service to the Allies. Wilhelm journeyed to Bökerhof a second time, hoping to cull more treasures from the von Haxthausen sisters. The household, he wrote to Jacob shortly after his arrival in Böker-hof, was positively bursting with "fairy tales, songs and legends, old sayings," as if the fire for collecting had been stoked by the promise of peace. "I've written down a very good portion," Wilhelm told his brother, but there was so much material to gather from his generous collaborators that he would "have to stay here 4–6 weeks in order to copy it all out with care and precision."[11]

On this second visit to Bökerhof, Wilhelm was also sur-prised to meet two more ladies who demonstrated an impressive knowledge of folklore: Jenny and Annette von Droste-Hülshoff, relatives of the von Haxthausen siblings. The two girls, and "es-pecially the youngest Annette," Wilhelm wrote to Jacob, knew far more fairy tales than anyone else. But Wilhelm did not warm easily to Annette. He thought she was "pushy and unpleasant," and reported that he "couldn't come to any sort of understand-ing with her." Annette had been born prematurely, which, he rea-soned, was the cause of her difficult behavior. "She wanted to radiate her brilliance constantly," he criticized, "and jumped from one topic to the next, but she truly promised to copy down everything that she knows and to send it."[12]

Though he was nine years older than Annette at the time of their first meeting, Wilhelm fell into an immature competition with her, afraid as he was of her wild intellect. A year later, he was still rattled by her person. He even wrote to tell a colleague that he had "recently had a truly fantastic and frightening dream about Miss Nette." In the dream, she "was cloaked completely in a dark purple flame and, one after another, pulled single hairs [from her head], flinging them at me through the air." The hairs, he added, "transformed themselves into arrows," which "could have easily made me blind."[13]

Eighteen-year-old Jenny, on the other hand, was the complete opposite of her precocious sister. She was "gentle and quiet," Wilhelm reported, pitting the two girls against one another in the same fashion that he had done with Friederike Mannel and Fränz Brentano. Although Jenny promised Wilhelm that she would see to it that Annette kept her word about writing down the tales, her mediating role between the two could not avert a feud that would last for years.[14]

Of all the women at Bökerhof, Wilhelm became most intimate with Jenny von Droste-Hülshoff. One story that we know she contributed to the Grimm anthology was called "The Worn Out Dancing Shoes,"[15] a rags-to-riches tale about a poor man's transcendence of class and social rank. The narrative also features the character of the soldier protagonist who, having been wounded in the war, is no longer of use to his army. "Once upon a time," the story goes, "there was a king who had twelve daughters, one more beautiful than the next." The princesses, we learn, sleep in a chamber together on twelve beds. Each night, when they go to bed, the door to their room is locked and barred, and yet, every morning the palace wakes up to find the princesses' shoes entirely worn out from dancing. Naturally, the mystery drives the girls' father crazy, and he declares that he who discovers how the disobedient girls escape the palace each night may choose the daughter of his liking for a wife. If the suitor fails to solve the puzzle, however, he will lose his head.

At first, a royal prince takes a stab at winning a wife, but the twelve ladies trick him by slipping a sleeping potion into his wine at bedtime. Sure enough, he snores right through their escapades, and the next morning the king finds his daughters' shoes full of holes again. The story then announces the prince's unhappy fate: "Off with his head!"

Then it happens that a poor soldier who can no longer serve his army arrives in the city. On his way there, he encounters an old woman who asks him where he is going. "I don't really know myself," the soldier answers, "but I'd love to become king and find out where the king's daughters dance away their shoes." "Ay! That isn't so difficult," the old woman exclaims. "All you have to do is not drink the wine they will bring you in the evening and pretend that you are fast asleep." Then she gives the soldier a magic cloak that makes him invisible. If he heeds the old woman's instructions, he will be able to follow the twelve sisters and discover where they go each night.

The plan works. Upon arriving at the castle, the soldier is given quarters in a room adjacent to the princesses' bedchamber. When it's time to go to sleep, he pretends to drink the doctored wine and feigns a sudden sleep, to which he adds loud snores. When the princesses hear his snoring, they laugh and chortle with glee because the young soldier, like the prince who failed before him, will surely lose his life. Then, the story reads, they "all got out of bed, threw open closets and trunks and boxes, took out magnificent clothes, made themselves up before the mirror and pranced around," happily anticipating the dance. After making sure the soldier is still asleep, the oldest sister goes to her own bed and knocks on the headboard. Suddenly, the bed sinks down into the earth and a trapdoor opens. The soldier secretly watches the girls climb down, one after the other. Then, putting on his magic cloak, he follows them into their secret subterranean place.

At the bottom is "a wondrous arbor," like the path of arching trees at Bökerhof where Wilhelm heard his first story from Anna von Haxthausen and where he surely took many walks with his friend Jenny. The leaves on the trees in the magical arbor of the story "were made of silver and shone and sparkled." Wanting to bring back proof of this enchanted land to the king, the soldier breaks a branch from one of the lovely trees. Then he follows the twelve princesses to yet another arbor lined with trees of gold, then to a third made of diamonds. Each time, he takes a branch.

Finally, the sisters reach a castle where twelve handsome princes await them. Their merrymaking is raucous, and the couples dance and drink wine to their hearts' abandon. By three in the morning, however, "all their shoes had holes in them and they had to stop." While the princesses bid their beloved princes farewell, promising to return the following night, the soldier runs ahead and makes it back to the ladies' bedroom in the palace just in the nick of time. Lying down in his own bed, he pretends to be asleep. When the girls arrive home, they are happy to see that the soldier has not moved an inch and knows nothing of their journey. "Then they took off their beautiful clothes, put them away, and placed their danced out shoes under their beds and lay down to sleep."

The next morning, the soldier presents the branches of the precious trees to the king. The king sends for the princesses immediately, and sternly questions them. Seeing that "they had been betrayed and that denying was of no help," the princesses confess everything to their father. The soldier wins his prize and takes the eldest as his bride.

For Wilhelm Grimm, the many ladies of the Romantic intellectual circle at Bökerhof were something like the princesses in "The Worn Out Dancing Shoes," privileged aristocrats who possessed special abilities that, like the poor soldier, he did not witness often in women of his own social class. In a sense, Wilhelm possessed a secret view of the von Haxthausen sisters' most intimate lives as educated ladies of the upper social strata who possessed far more power than most women of the age. And perhaps, one among them, "gentle and quiet" Jenny von Droste-Hülshoff just might become his bride, for during the visit to Bökerhof that summer of 1813, something more than a friendship had kindled between the two. In her diary, Jenny later confessed a passion for Wilhelm, after seeing him briefly on a trip to Kassel with her sister Annette. She wrote that Wilhelm was "so dear" that she "only took notice of him and [didn't] know what any of the others were doing." He also spoke intimate words to her and reminded her of his happy visit to Bökerhof, where they had first met, and of the special place where they had "bid one another farewell." When it was time for Jenny and Annette to leave Kassel, the same "bitter hour of departure" that Jenny had felt on the day that Wilhelm had departed from Bökerhof struck again. "Wilhelm kissed Nette's hand . . . then mine," she wrote, "but we both didn't say a thing to one another. I had no thoughts whatsoever in that moment, and had he said something to me, I would not have understood it."[16]

10

THE GOOSE MAID

NONE OF THE YOUNG LADIES WHO CONTRIBUTED STORIES to the Grimm anthology, whether they were of the middle or aristocratic class, fit the picture of the yarn-telling old peasant maid, but in the spring of 1813, the closest thing to the brothers' ideal of the preserver of folk culture emerged in the person of Dorothea Viehmann. "We now have a splendid source," Wilhelm wrote to his brother Ferdinand about their new discovery, "an old woman from Zwern who knows unbelievably much and who is good at storytelling." She had "an intelligent face and, more than most farming people, a sharp, fine bearing," as Wilhelm described the woman. "She comes to visit at least once a week and unleashes [her stories]. We take turns transcribing her for 3–4 hours at a time, and by now have [made] such lovely progress that we could probably deliver a second volume. The war alone is what's holding everything up."[1]

The war had certainly taken a toll on the Viehmann family. Zwern, the small village where they lived, was located just outside of Kassel, and Dorothea, in an effort to make ends meet, often walked into the city to sell vegetables from her garden. But she was by no means a farmer, as Wilhelm had described her in his letter to Ferdinand. When Dorothea's father, Johann Friedrich Isaak Pierson, had married her mother, he had taken on the family business, an old Hessian inn outside of Kassel called the *Knallhütte.* Together, the couple raised their children there.

Dorothea was born in 1755. As a young girl, she probably picked up some of her first stories from the coachmen and cargo haulers who journeyed through the region and stayed at the inn. Her mother, Martha Getrud, was also a likely early source for her daughter's expansive repertoire. In 1777, at the age of twenty-two, Dorothea married Niklaus Viehmann, who was a tailor. Thus, though the Viehmanns were not common peasants, neither were they from the bourgeoisie. In straddling the line of so-called middle-class respectability, they suffered tremendous loss and privation during the French Revolution and the Napoleonic Wars as they struggled to raise their six children; indeed, the Viehmanns, along with many other Hessians, were forced to pay the heavy taxes levied by Napoleon to cover France's insurmountable war debt.

The very location of Dorothea's childhood home, the *Knallhütte,* had even been the tragic site of a battle in April 1809, when thousands of Hessians had banded together in a wave of angry resistance against Jerôme Bonaparte. Wanting to restore their old lives of relative stability under their former monarch, Elector Wilhelm I, they demanded that their sovereign be returned to the throne. "On Saturday, not far from here in Old Hesse," Jacob had written to a colleague about the conflict, "a resistance broke out, led by the commandant of the royal guard of riflemen." But the army that had assembled itself was easily defeated by Jerôme's artillery forces, and Jacob expressed the pain he felt at seeing Germans who had been forcefully conscripted into the French army arrest their fellow Hessians. "I will never in my life forget a wagon upon which five farmers sat, close to one another, side by side, completely still," he wrote. He went on to describe their blonde hair, and how they sat quietly and stared back at the hoard of people who watched them being carted off to prison. "One can only hope," he added, that the captives "wouldn't be treated with great severity.²" In addition to his position as court librarian for Jerôme, Jacob had also been assigned as the only German ministerial advisor to the king's cabinet. He knew Jerôme more intimately than most Hessians and hoped the king would show his merciful side. The damage to citizens' morale and property, however, ran deep. During the Westphalian regime, Dorothea Viehmann's family lost nearly all their possessions, and by the time Jacob and Wilhelm met her in 1813, she was in her mid-fifties and toiling to earn whatever she could for the family purse.

Viehmann possessed a savant-like ability in telling unusually compelling fairy tales. It was her way of overcoming the hardship that so many years of privation had placed upon her shoulders. She took pride in this gift, and her weekly visits to the Grimms' home were occasions she savored. Jacob and Wilhelm showered her with luxuries she could never afford for herself: a cup of coffee, a glass of wine. Sometimes they gave her tip money. Out on the streets, while selling her vegetables, she would gossip with townsfolk about how royally the brothers had treated her. They had even given her a silver spoon to stir her coffee with!

Viehmann's method of telling tales suited Jacob and Wilhelm's editorial needs to perfection. She could, if asked to do so, stop mid-sentence and recount the previous segment of a story word for word. All the while, she maintained a narrative poise that was enthralling. In volume two of the *Children's and Household Fairy Tales*, the brothers honored her with pride of place, even crediting Viehmann by name in the foreword. Yet, in their homage, they falsely described her as a "farmer's wife."[3]

The truth of the matter was that Viehmann's family history was not unlike that of the Hassenpflugs. They were Huguenots, and many of the tales Dorothea added to the Grimm anthology betrayed French provenances. Her "Cinderella," for example, had strong affinities with two versions of the tale published in the eighteenth century, one by Charles Perrault, the other by Madame d'Alonoy. The motif of the glass slipper, used as a means of divining the identity of the prince's true love, dates even further back and appears in Giambattista Basile's *Pentamerone*, a collection of Neapolitan folk tales published in 1637.[4]

If the female collaborators' identities in the first volume of the fairy tales had been concealed, Dorothea Viehmann's was overtly idealized in the second. "This woman," the Grimms' foreword described her, was "still robust," and possessed "a sturdy and pleasant face" that "gazed out brightly and crisply from her eyes." She was "probably beautiful in her youth" and had "preserved these old legends firmly in her memory." Whenever Dorothea Viehmann told stories, she was, as the brothers sang her praises, "deliberate, confident and extremely alive," taking great joy in her craft.

Viehmann's total contribution to the *Children's and Household Fairy Tales* amounted to more than forty stories. Although some tales were completely new to the anthology, others represented variations of tales that the Grimms had already gathered from their lady friends in Allendorf, Kassel, and Bökerhof. Thus, some of Viehmann's original submissions were fully preserved in the second volume, but others were partially fused with previous versions edited by Wilhelm, in a second edition of the *Children's and Household Fairy Tales*, volumes one and two combined, published in 1819. One example of Wilhelm's editorial process of integrating more than one version of a story into a reconstructed narrative was the tale of "Cinderella." The first version, published in volume one in 1812, had been transcribed from the legendary fairy tale lady of Marburg, whom Lotte Grimm—at least in Wilhelm's eyes—had miserably failed at securing the confidences of. Later, Wilhelm took Viehmann's telling of the story and combined it with the Marburg version.

Because Dorothea Viehmann demonstrated such genius in the genre, the collaboration with her was the most intense and meaningful the brothers had yet experienced, so much so that they documented the process of their work with her in great detail. When she began telling a story, they reported in the foreword to volume two, she did it freely, extemporaneously, and shined in the performance. Then, if asked to do so, Viehmann would repeat the tale "once more, slowly, so that with a little bit of practice one [could] transcribe her." The approach suited the Grimms' theoretical program for faithful documentation: "Much is preserved word for word in this way," they wrote in assuring their readers of the unmistaken "truth" of Viehmann's stories. The brothers even went so far as to admonish potential detractors who might suspect that a "slight distortion of transmission" and a "laziness in the preservation" of the oral telling were part of the complex process of bringing what was spoken aloud into print on the page.[5] This was a most urgent point for them to make, and it betrayed something about Viehmann's ingenuity. Her astounding memory played an extremely important role, for whenever she doubled back to repeat part of a story during transcription, she never changed the content; indeed, it was as if she were performing a well-memorized dramatic role.

Though many of the stories Viehmann contributed to the Grimm anthologies are relatively unknown today, they are arguably some of the most unusual and imaginative, and their titles are suggestive of these traits: "The Devil with Three Golden Hairs," "Loyal Johannes," "Little Tiller," and "Doctor Know It All." One favorite of the brothers was "The Goose Maid,"[6] a tale of switched identities. On one of her visits to the Grimm home, Viehmann opened this story with a stock character found in many a fairy tale: the widow-mother. "There once lived an old queen whose husband had died many years ago,"

Dorothea narrated as Jacob took down her words. The queen, we learn, has a lovely daughter who is promised to a prince in a faraway land. As the time approaches for the wedding, "the old woman packed many precious objects and jewelry: gold and silver, chalices and gems, in short, everything that belonged to a royal dowry, for she loved her child with all her heart." The queen also gives the princess a chambermaid to bring along on the journey to her new home. Each girl is provided with a horse for the trip, but the princess's horse is special. His name is Falada, and he possesses the magic power of speech.

"When the hour of departure arrived," the story continues, "the old mother retired to her sleeping chambers, took out a small knife, and cut herself in the finger so that she bled." The queen then holds a white cloth beneath the cut, allowing three drops to fall into it. Then, bidding her daughter farewell, she presses the handkerchief into her hand, telling the princess to watch over it with care, for the cloth could help her in an hour of need. Just as in earlier centuries it was believed that a strand of hair or even saliva from another person possessed shielding powers, these drops of mother's blood become a protective charm for the princess.[7]

And so mother and daughter take leave from one another in sadness. The princess tucks the little cloth into her breast, mounts her horse, and sets off to join her groom in the distant kingdom. As she is riding, she begins to feel "a hot thirst," the story tells us, and calls to her chambermaid. "Get down and dip some water for me from the brook with my chalice," she commands. But the chambermaid is a cheeky girl. "Ay," she replies, "get down yourself, lean over the water, and drink. I don't want to be your maid!" The princess is so parched that she doesn't argue with the girl. She dismounts, and, foregoing drinking from her golden chalice, sips directly from the brook on her hands and knees. By allowing her servant such rudeness, she has demeaned her royal rank and rightful place in the feudal structure. The princess sighs in frustration: "Ach, God!" Her lamentation causes the three drops of blood inside the handkerchief to speak aloud to her. "If your mother knew about this," they tell her, "her heart would burst."

In spite of the protective charm, the princess is entirely bullied by her maid. She mounts her horse again, and they ride on for miles, the hot sun beating down. Soon, the same scenario repeats itself, this time at a waterfall. "Ach, God!" the princess sighs again as she is drinking the water, and the drops of blood remind her of how heartbroken her mother would be if she knew what was happening. This time while the princess is drinking, the handkerchief falls into the water and drifts away. She doesn't notice it, but the chambermaid sees what has happened and is very pleased. With the protective charm forever lost, she can have her way with the princess still more.

Next, the impudent maid steals her lady's magic horse, Falada. "I belong on top of Falada, and you belong on top of my old nag," she instructs. She also insists that they exchange clothes: The maid then dons the princess's finery and leaves her mistress with her own rags. The princess's true identity is now completely concealed, and the maid forces her to swear, under the threat of death, that she will tell no one of the switch. Then the two girls ride off together and head toward the castle in the distance, the chambermaid on Falada, the princess on the "inferior steed."

When they arrive at the palace, the mean chambermaid manages to dupe the entire court into thinking that she is the prince's bride. The true princess is taken in as a servant and given the chore of watching over the geese. Every morning, when she brings the birds out to a field to feed, she must take a boy named "little Conrad" with her. Fearing that the magical speaking horse, Falada, might give away her mistress's true identity, the wicked chambermaid demands that the prince have the horse's head chopped off. When our heroine discovers this awful plan, she pays the stable boy a gold piece to hang poor Falada's head above the city gate, under which she and little Conrad must pass each morning with the geese on their way to the field.

Early the next day, when the princess and little Conrad are driving the geese through the gate, she looks up at the horse's head, and, as they pass beneath, she says: "Oh, Falada, hanging up above." The horse's head answers her, "Oh, my lady princess, walking down below, if your mother knew of this her heart would break in two!"

Then the princess and little Conrad continue on their way. When they reach a meadow, the princess sits down and begins to undo her braids. Seeing that the girl's hair is "precious silver" and gleams brilliantly in the sun (a sign of her royal birth), little Conrad tries to pluck a hair from her head. But the girl casts a spell on the boy:

Blow! Blow! Little wind,
carry Conrad's hat away,
and make him go chasing after it
until I've braided and plaited
and made myself new again.

Immediately, a strong wind kicks up and sends little Conrad running after his hat, long enough for the princess to finish braiding her hair and so protect it from the boy's clutches.

The following day, the princess and little Conrad repeat the same routine. Falada and the girl have their cryptic dialogue at the city gate, and little Conrad is sent off across the meadow to chase his hat in the wind. Feeling angry, the boy goes to the prince's father and tells him of his frustration with the goose maid. The king finds Conrad's story mysterious and decides to follow the girl out to the field the next morning. Upon seeing with his own eyes exactly what little Conrad has told him, the king wants some answers. He calls for the girl and asks her why she does so many curious things. "I may not tell you or any other person," she fearfully replies, "otherwise I will lose my life." But the king presses her. "If you can't tell me," he says, "then you can tell it to the oven." The girl agrees to this idea and, crawling inside the oven, she "emptie[s] her entire heart out," and tells "everything that had happened to her and how she had been betrayed by the evil chambermaid." The oven, we read, happens to have a hole in the top of it, so it is convenient for the king to eavesdrop on the girl. Thus, he "overhear[s] her fate word for word."

Upon discovering the goose maid's true identity, the king immediately orders royal clothing for her and directs her to don the finery. The moment she does so, her wondrous beauty shines forth. Then the king calls for his son and reveals the deceptive story of his bride, who was "nothing more than a chambermaid." Beholding the real princess's "beauty and virtue," the prince is "happy in his heart." Yet, as in so many fairy tales, justice is served on a rather brutal note. In punishment, the wicked chambermaid is stripped "bare naked" and locked inside a barrel studded on the inside with sharp spikes; then she is dragged through the streets behind a wagon until she dies. Jacob and Wilhelm's hearts soared when they heard Viehmann's "Goose Maid" and other such intriguing stories; indeed, along with the scores of wonderful tales streaming in from Bökerhof, Dorothea's additions now made a second volume a certainty.

On June 13, 1813, she shared another unusual tale that plays with masked identities. It was called "Doctor Know It All," a comical *Schwankmärchen*.[8] Fairy tales of this genre often feature a simpleton, generally male, who unwittingly achieves great fame and fortune through a string of well-intentioned but misguided deeds. The story humorously subverts the boundaries that separate people by class, wealth, and education by poking fun at societal rank. This was a very fitting narrative at a time when social standing had become an obsession with most Europeans, who saw the era of Napoleon drawing to a close and wondered about their political future and rights as citizens. The old monarchs who were in power before Bonaparte began forging new plans to seize control of most of the Continent, playing their game of political chess in what would become the new Europe. At the same time, common citizens still inspired by the French Revolution were pressing for greater self-representation than they had enjoyed before Napoleon's invasions.

"Once there was a poor farmer by the name of Crab [who] drove a load of wood with two oxen into the city and sold it to a doctor for two *Thaler*," the beginning of "Doctor Know It All" tells us. While the money is being paid out to the poor farmer, the doctor is just sitting down for a meal. Seeing "all the lovely things" the wealthy doctor is about to eat and drink, the farmer wishes with all his heart that he, too, might have the same luxuries. After standing there watching the prosperous man dine for a while, the poor man finally asks how he might become a doctor. "Oh, yes," the man answers him, "that's easily done. First of all, buy yourself an ABC book, just like this one, with a [picture of a] cock-hen inside. Second, turn your wagon and your two oxen into money, and get yourself some clothes and whatever else you need for doctoring. Third, have a sign painted with the words: 'I Am Doctor Know It All,' and nail it above your house door."

The poor man does everything the doctor tells him, and after practicing his new vocation for a while, he is approached by a rich man who has been robbed of a great deal of money. The rich man wants to catch the thief, so he asks Doctor Know It All to journey to his palace to help find the offender. Doctor Know It All agrees to go; but, he says, his wife, Grethe must come too. The rich man agrees to this and brings the husband

and wife to his palace. When they arrive there, the table is being set for a nice meal. "You should eat first," the rich man says. "Yes," Doctor Know It All eagerly agrees, "but my wife Grethe [should eat], too."

While they're dining, a servant comes into the room carrying a bowl of lovely food. Seeing the scrumptious dish, the farmer elbows his wife. "Grethe, that was the first," he says, meaning it is the first course of the meal. The servant, however, thinks that Doctor Know It All means that he was the first thief, and because "he indeed was, he became afraid." Outside, in the servant's hall, the thief tells his comrades about Doctor Know It All's secret knowledge. "We're in for trouble. He said that I was the first." The routine repeats itself with a second, and a third, and a fourth servant, each of them terrified that they will be discovered by the wise doctor. After a series of misspoken words and hilarious turns of phrase, Doctor Know It All eventually finds where the money is stashed, but he doesn't reveal the thieves' true identities, just as he never reveals his own. Instead, he cashes in by collecting a bribe from the thieves and a reward from the rich man.

The distortion of identity is a strong theme in several of Dorothea Viehmann's stories. The lesson of "Doctor Know It All" is that willfully masking one's own persona can be exceedingly profitable. On another note, "The Goose Maid" teaches just the opposite: falling victim to another's devious attempts at obscuring one's own identity can be exceedingly damaging. Something about Dorothea Viehmann was different from all the other female contributors the brothers Grimm had known. She satisfied a deep theoretical need, a Romantic literary conceit, that the educated daughters of the German middle class and aristocracy simply could not. But the Grimms had created an identity for Viehmann that was inaccurate. Though she wasn't as literate as her female co-collaborators of the von Haxthausen and von Droste-Hülshoff families, she had more education than the brothers let on, and she certainly wasn't a peasant farmer. Being of Huguenot heritage, Viehmann spoke French relatively well, yet her stories, though they possessed French provenances, were reframed by the Grimms as "quintessentially Hessian" in their foreword to volume two of the fairy tales.[9]

As Germans' hope for independence soared in light of Napoleon's imminent defeat, the veiling of Dorothea Vieh-mann in the *Children's and Household Fairy Tales* was an unconscious move that was influenced by patriotic emotion on the part of Jacob and Wilhelm. They had obscured their story-telling friend so that they could fit her more properly into the ideals and convictions they were feeling for their native land in the moment of its potential rebirth.

11

THE END OF AN ERA

R UMOR HAD SPREAD THROUGHOUT KASSEL THAT KING
Jerôme, fearing a sudden attack on his sovereignty at any
moment, had given orders for a carriage and horses to be held
ready round the clock in case he needed to make a quick escape.
It was also known that, since as early as the spring of 1813, the
Pallais Bellevue, Jerôme's residence in the city, was being emp-
tied of its most valuable articles, which were then transported
secretly to France.

The inevitable did come to pass. On September 28, 1814,
Chernichev, a great Russian general, leading an army of Cos-
sacks, opened fire on the city in a battle against French troops
commanded by General Allix. In the blink of an eye, a mass of

Hessian citizens rose up and joined the Russians, successfully forcing the French to relinquish the city. "On that morning," Ludwig Grimm's future wife wrote in her diary, "three people were killed by cannon balls: (1) a porcelain mender, (2) a shepherd woman, and (3) gardener Meiss's son."[1] Jerôme Bonaparte immediately fled to Marburg. One month later, he attempted to regain control of Kassel, but failed; and by October 26, he had been permanently removed from Hesse, his seven-year reign now at an end.

Jacob wrote to his friend Arnim about the long-anticipated evacuation of the French from his city. "You'd hardly believe how [they] have withdrawn from us," he exclaimed, "so effortlessly and with nearly no sensation." The only Frenchman in Jerôme's court who was "a loyal and especially kind man" was nowhere to be found in the final days. "Other than he," Jacob wrote, "I know of not one soul, among all the high and low ranked people, that I ever respected or that I might pity now." His service to the French king "had become ever more meaningless" in the final year. He went on: "The library was packed up and moved out. I attended the meetings of the City Council only twice or three times in a single year, and not only I, but other colleagues as well, remained aloof without reprimand, so little did our superiors have an eye on order in the whole matter."[2]

In the same letter, Jacob described the banished king as vain and foolish and "caught up in a constant, doubly debauched game of aping the Emperor," his brother Napoleon. Jerôme's biggest mistake as king, however, was his inability to show a serious "love and understanding" of his people.[3] In all his seven years in Hesse, the king had never learned to speak the German language, a true embarrassment from Jacob's standpoint, for his scholarship with Wilhelm had brought him to the conclusion that language had the power to transcend national differences and, in doing so, to bring people together. The fairy tales themselves, with their long oral tradition, their narrative malleability, and the ease with which they seemed to move across borders in a variety of tongues and dialects, were proof of this.

In less than a month after Jerôme's departure from Kassel, Hesse's former regent, Elector Wilhelm, returned from exile to the city with his wife, Wilhelmine Karoline. They arrived in grand display, moving in procession through the center of the city as the townsfolk ran into the streets and rejoiced. Jacob, Wilhelm, and Lotte were especially jubilant, for their beloved Aunt Henriette had returned home to them again.

Wilhelm I immediately set to work assembling a Hessian army that would join the Allies against Napoleon in a march on Paris. Jacob was assigned to join the campaign as secretary to Count Keller, the Hessian representative to the Grand Allied Headquarters. Though he did not relish the idea of traveling in such chaotic times because it would significantly interrupt his research, Jacob felt it was his duty to serve in the German war of liberation against those who had encroached upon his home, his language, and his daily way of life for so long. Meanwhile, Ludwig and Karl Grimm were serving in the Hessian army, and Wilhelm offered the proceeds of a second edition of his publication of *Poor Henry* to assist in outfitting newly recruited volunteers to the forces.

Hessian women prepared their husbands, sons, and brothers for the war by knitting warm clothing and sewing and repairing garments. On a cold winter day in 1814, just after the New Year, Lotte Grimm packed her brother Jacob's bags for his long journey into enemy territory. Aunt Zimmer did her bit, too, sending her nephew into the field with a satchel of supplies she had made and purchased, including a pair of woolen galoshes.

Jacob traveled with the Grand Allied Headquarters first to Frankfurt, then on to Karlsruhe and Rastadt. With each mile, the trip became more demanding and dangerous. The Allied delegation often had to separate into small groups of traveling parties to avoid enemy gunfire and attacks, and the frigid winter air cut to the bone during the long hours of carriage travel. Jacob wore the woolen galoshes that Henriette had given him, but, to his dismay, he accidentally left them behind in Frankfurt. Even worse than the cold was the blinding reflection of the sun on the snow-covered fields in the long stretches of countryside they traversed. It made Jacob fearful of losing his vision.

If the physical discomforts weren't enough, Jacob also witnessed countless acts of petty thievery and violence among their own Allied forces, and, when the delegation had reached enemy soil, he was appalled to learn that Allied soldiers had raped and abused French women in many of the small villages they had encamped in. Ruffian soldiers who had suffered long years at war felt justified in treating the French in this way; but, unlike the soldiers' harsh morality, which was comparable to that of some of the fairy tales, Jacob's perception of justice was not the Biblical revenge that calls for an "eye for an eye." "One speaks of peace," he wrote gloomily to Wilhelm from the road. "I only wish that [we] could be true to [ourselves] and positively liberate everything that Germany is." After that, he wrote, the Allies should simply let the French be. Otherwise, he warned, the Allies would simply "do the same to them" that they had "suffered from them."[4]

The paradox of serving Count Keller, an aristocratic minister of high privilege, when poverty and destruction awaited them in every small town they traveled through, also weighed upon Jacob's conscience. High-ranking officials in the delegation held extravagant parties and dinners, which Jacob desperately tried to avoid attending. Surrounded by the decadence, he was beginning to feel isolated and homesick. From Basel, he reported that he had gone to the theater "in order to forget [his] loneliness," but the plays and the actors were "sincerely poor." The only thing that had made an impression on him were the Russian officers in the audience who "clapped incessantly, either because they didn't understand a thing or because they wanted to make a bit of fun for themselves."[5] How very strange that so many foreigners would come together in an effort such as this, the liberation of Europe from the Bonapartes.

Back at home, Wilhelm attempted to keep pace with their research projects and efforts on the fairy tale anthology, but there were too many interruptions during the day. Troops from various European armies moved in and out of Kassel in a constant flow, and they took up quarters in citizens' homes, including the Grimms' apartment. Alone with only Lotte for company, Wilhelm was beginning to miss Jacob, too. "It's morning, and as usual, the tea machine is boiling," he wrote, reminding Jacob of their cozy domestic routines. "Beside me is your table with its papers, and your chair [is standing] before it." As was true of the separations between the brothers in the past, this was a painful time. The long years of collaboration on the fairy tales had bound Jacob and Wilhelm together in every aspect of their lives. "After I sadly watched your lantern travel up the street like a star until it disappeared around the corner," Wilhelm wrote of his brother's departure from Kassel, "we [Wilhelm and Lotte] sat quietly" together in the house.[6]

In his daily activities, Wilhelm was now surrounded entirely by women. Aunt Zimmer had moved into her new quarters in the city: "The house is very well appointed and the Electress is thoroughly satisfied." As she unpacked her things, Henriette brought out many "marvelous flannels" and "silk fabrics for vests" for Jacob and Wilhelm. "She is far too good, how she has always thought about and cared for us," Wilhelm wrote.[7] Henriette was now sixty-six years old and still faithfully serving her lady, the electress. Wilhelm visited his aunt devotedly, every other day, and though he had asked Lotte to do the same, she disregarded his wishes. Little had changed in the brothers' domestic opinion of their sister. Lotte's distance regarding Henriette aggravated Wilhelm to no end, and when she had packed his bags for the journey to France, Jacob complained in a letter from Rastadt that she had not included his good silk pants.

Dortchen Wild was nineteen years old now and a true and constant element of the Grimm family. Her name came up in the brothers' letters with more frequency than Lotte's. "Send Dortchen my warm greetings," Jacob would often write. "Dortchen says hello," Wilhelm would answer in return. On one occasion, Wilhelm reported that Dortchen had bought them a new set of knives for the kitchen. On his birthday, she had baked him a cake and had given him some lovely flowers. He always mentioned when she had taken ill and detailed to Jacob how long she had needed to stay in bed. Her health had deteriorated since the recent death of her mother, whom Dortchen nursed to her dying day. Now Dortchen's father, Rudolf, had fallen ill with dropsy. With "old man Wild" so sick, Wilhelm wrote to Jacob, Dortchen had a lot to do.[8] As the only daughter left in the household—the others had married and moved out—she often stayed up until one or two in the morning so that she could catch up on the day's work.

In spite of her responsibilities at home, Dortchen managed to knit six pairs of socks for Ludwig Grimm to take with him to the field. Ludwig and Karl had just arrived in Kassel with their new regiment. "When it came to the swearing in," Wilhelm wrote of the church service held in honor of the Hessian army the day before his brothers marched into battle, "all the farmers solemnly and reverently raised their hands," while "the finer people looked as if they were ashamed of themselves."[9] The following morning, Wilhelm marched through the streets of Kassel side-by-side with Ludwig and his unit as it made its way for the city gates. They walked all the way to Poplar Alley together, he told Jacob, where they kissed each other goodbye. Wilhelm also managed to find Karl in the throng and bid him farewell. "God keep them both," he wrote, hoping their youngest brothers would return home safely.[10]

Arriving in Chaumont on March 19, Jacob's letters began to show signs of depressing fatigue for the unending horrors he was presented with. "One must take a closer look at what the soldier must endure," he wrote to Wilhelm. Illness, hospital, and imprisonment were the most horrible things a common soldier suffered in the ugliness of war. Recently, he had seen a young officer lying in the middle of the thoroughfare while carriages and marching troops simply maneuvered around him. Some passed by indifferently, and no one stopped to help the boy, leaving Jacob to wonder whether later that night he had died right there beneath the open sky without being buried.[11]

The previous summer, Dorothea Viehmann had added an unusual tale to the brothers' anthology titled "The Three Army Surgeons."[12] It is one of the few stories that make reference to the theme of war, and it involves gruesome amputations. But unlike the amputations the heroine who loses her hands in "The Maiden with No Hands" suffers, those in "The Three Army Surgeons" are not symbolic of a higher moral purpose. Instead, they are meant as burlesque commentary on the kind of class differences that Wilhelm perceived in the church before the Hessians had marched into battle, the hard truth being that it was far more likely for a common foot soldier, and not an army surgeon of the higher social class, to run the risk of losing an arm, a leg, or his life, in service to his country.

"Three army surgeons went out into the world thinking they had learned everything they could about their art," the story begins rather unassumingly. Arriving at an inn, the men decide to spend the night there. Upon hearing that they are surgeons, the innkeeper grows curious about their art and asks them to show him what they can do. The first surgeon boasts that he can cut off his own hand, then heal himself the following morning.

The second claims he can rip his own heart out, then put it back the next day. The third promises to poke out his own eyes, then restore his vision. But little does the innkeeper know that the three men possess a magic ointment. Wherever the strange salve is applied, the body heals instantly.

So, the story continues, the army surgeons "cut their hand, heart, and eyes from their bodies, just as they claimed they would." Then, putting everything together on a plate, the innkeeper gives the body parts to his kitchen maid and tells her to put them in the cupboard for safekeeping. The girl, we learn, has a secret lover who happens to be a soldier. That night, when everyone is sleeping, the soldier—it's a given that he is poor and without means—sneaks into the inn for a free meal. When he arrives there, the maid unlocks the cupboard and fetches something for him to eat. But her passion for her man makes the maid a little forgetful, and she doesn't close the cupboard door behind her. Sitting down beside him at the table, the girl watches her beloved eat, and soon the two lose themselves in conversation. Just then, the house cat comes slinking into the kitchen and finds the cupboard door wide open. Snatching up the hand, the heart, and the eyes on the plate, the bad cat dashes out of the house. When the maid goes to clean up after her boyfriend's meal, she discovers, to her dismay, an empty plate in the cupboard. "Ach! Poor maid that I am! What will I do?" she cries.

The soldier comes to her rescue. "Just give me a sharp knife," he tells her. "There is a thief hanging in the gallows. I'll go and cut off his hand. Which [hand] was it, then?" he asks. "The right one," the maid replies. And so, the soldier runs off to the gallows and cuts the hand off "the poor sinner" and brings it back to his girlfriend. Then the soldier spies the cat slinking about, and he makes a grab for the animal and gouges its eyes out. Now all that's left to drum up in this bizarre scavenger hunt is a heart. "Didn't you do your butchering today?" the soldier asks the kitchen maid, "and have you not some pork in the cellar?" The girl answers yes. "Well, that's good," he replies, and off he goes to find the pig's heart. Once all the body parts are assembled, the kitchen maid puts them onto the plate, locks them up in the cupboard and, after kissing her beau goodbye, rests easily through the night.

As one might expect, the plot of the missing body parts in "The Three Army Surgeons" begins to thicken. The next morning, the innkeeper brings the three doctors the plate with their alleged belongings on it. The first surgeon puts the thief's hand to his wrist, rubs it with the magic ointment, and, lo and behold, the hand fuses itself to his arm. The second man stuffs the cat's eyes into his empty sockets, applies the ointment, and, miraculously, his vision is restored. Finally, the third surgeon puts the pig's heart inside his chest. In wonderment, the innkeeper says he's never seen such a thing in all his life and promises to spread the word and make the three surgeons famous.

The doctors, however, begin to behave quite strangely. The one with the pig's heart, we read, wanders off to a corner and, unable to help himself, "sniff[s] around [there] as pigs do." Then he scurries off to the thickest mud he can find and rolls around in it. Things don't go too well for the second surgeon, either. Rubbing his eyes in puzzlement, he says, "Comrades, what is it? These aren't my eyes. I can't see a thing. Show me the way, so that I don't stumble." Thus, the three strange invalids depart and walk, with great effort, almost like injured foot soldiers on a long march in the field, until they reach the next inn. Inside, they see a rich man counting his money at a table in the corner. The surgeon with the thief's hand begins to feel a twitching in his fingers and makes a grab for the man's money. His companions are astonished and scold him bitterly. "Oh," he pleads with them, "I can't help it!"

That night, when the three men lie down to sleep, we finally learn about the third surgeon's (the one with the cat's eyes) unlucky fate. The room they're sleeping in is "so dark," the story puns, "that you couldn't see your own hand before your eyes." Suddenly, the man cries out to the others. "Brothers, look! Can you see the little white mice scurrying around?"

By now, the surgeons are beginning to realize that something is not right with them. Hoping to find answers, they return to the inn where everything had gone so awry. When they tell their story to the innkeeper, he blames the kitchen maid and calls out for the girl. The maid, however, sees trouble brewing and slips out the back door, never to return again. To make up for the surgeons' losses, the innkeeper must give the three men all his money and everything he owns. It's enough wealth to last their entire lives, but, the story concludes, "they would have rather had their right parts." As we saw in "Doctor Know It All," a man of medicine is always a cut above in the given social strata. In "The Three Army Surgeons," a commoner, the poor soldier, rises above the army doctors by a comical twist of fate.

The story of "The Three Army Surgeons" strangely reflected the rising incidence of organ transplants that had begun
to take place in experimental medicine in Europe. With a war
going on, it was far easier for corpses to move through the black
market. Even Jacob, who by now had reached Paris with the Allied Headquarters, expressed a deep fear of dying far away from
home, terrified as he was about what might happen to his body
with no family member there to cart it off. A grave digger, he
wrote to Wilhelm, could easily sell off parts of it to doctors
who experimented in the dark arts.[13]

By the time the Allied Headquarters had reached Paris,
Napoleon Bonaparte had abdicated. With Jacob far away in
France for an indefinite period, Wilhelm tried to resume work
on the second volume of the fairy tales. He wrote to Jenny von
Droste-Hülshoff because he had heard from the von Haxthausens that Jenny had found and transcribed more fairy tales.
After all the "anguish and joy" of the final days of the war, and
with peace restored to Europe, he wrote to her, he was "using
these quiet hours" to "bring some order to what has been collected thus far." He asked Jenny to send him her new discoveries, and told her that he hoped to come to Bökerhof again that
summer, where he would have "the pleasure of thanking [her]
in person." In spite of all his gentility when it came to Jenny
von Droste-Hülshoff, Wilhelm still seemed to harbor a grudge
toward her sister Annette. Closing his letter, he sent regards to
"Miss Nette," but with a caveat: ". . . [only] if she still wants
to hear from me (just as we, now that the French have been
chased away, do not wish to be mean to anyone else either)."[14]

Wilhelm also announced to the von Haxthausen sisters his intention of pushing forward with publication of the scores of stories they had contributed over the past three years, and asked for new additions they might have. The response was swift. By the end of May 1814, he had received another package from Bökerhof. "Through your gift, madam," he wrote in thanks to Ludowine, "you have brought me unexpected joy." The stories, he wrote, were "doubly invaluable . . . in part because of their lovely, fairy-tale like content" and also because the sisters had delivered them in *Plattdeutsch*, a northern German dialect. For him, dialects imbued the stories with a naïveté and innocence that conjured up the true spirit of the *Volk*. He praised the sisters' fine work and added that their tales were "so well told," that he didn't "want to change a thing." Compared to the process of collecting for volume one of the fairy tales, which had been an arduous six years of "isolating and lonely" work for him and Jacob, this new volume "was developing much better" and, thanks to Ludowine and her sisters, would be published more swiftly. Their tales, he promised, would be "a decoration to volume two."[15]

That summer, Jacob returned home to Kassel to find the manuscript nearly complete. It was just as well, for soon he would depart again to join the Hessian delegation to Vienna, where the future of Europe after Bonaparte would be determined by all the powers of the Continent at the Vienna Congress. During his brief stay in Kassel, Jacob took time to visit their fairy tale queen, Dorothea Viehmann. Ludwig Grimm was also in Kassel, home from the war and suffering minor wounds;

he, too, visited Viehmann so that he could draw her portrait. His rendition of the storyteller appeared as the frontispiece of the 1819 edition of the *Children's and Household Fairy Tales.*

Because of his new diplomatic duties to Elector Wilhelm I, Jacob's involvement in the fairy tale anthologies was waning. Indeed, developments in Kassel following the war seemed to imply that the brothers' eight years of collecting from their women friends were coming to an end. The Grimms' landlord raised the rent of the family apartment in the Marktgasse exorbitantly high, which forced them to find a new home in the city. They took up quarters near the Pallais Bellevue so that Jacob could be in steady contact with the court, but the distance to the Wild household was much greater. Lotte was unhappy that she could no longer be in close proximity to Dortchen, though the families still remained in constant contact.

Many of the original contributors to the fairy tales were married now, busy with their husbands and households, giving birth, and adjusting to the new peace that had arrived in Europe. By the time Jacob left for Vienna in early September, the weekly reading circle was inactive, and the time for telling fairy tales had passed. Nearly overnight, it seemed, the new Europe was making new demands for new projects.

Volume two of the *Children's and Household Fairy Tales* was published in December 1814 and included seventy new stories. This number, however, in no way reflected the true magnitude of the contributions of the von Haxthausens, the von Droste-Hülshoffs, and Dorothea Viehmann, for some of the tales that had been shared would appear in later editions or as fusions of two or more versions. The women's total contribution was staggering: Seventy-five texts were submitted by the von Haxthausens and the von Droste-Hülshoffs at Bökerhof, and an additional forty came from Dorothea Viehmann.

In February 1815, Wilhelm was finally able to deliver a copy of the book to the ladies of Bökerhof. In a letter to Ludowine, he spoke highly of Dorothea Viehmann, but, he added, the "poor woman ha[d] been very ill . . . and ha[d] experienced great misfortune."[16] Wilhelm sent a copy of the tales to Jenny von Droste-Hülshoff that same day. "Finally, madam," he wrote, "I can thank you for your lovely contributions to our collection of fairy tales, which gave me so much pleasure and which arrived in the perfect moment." He added a few anecdotes about the final dramatic days of editing, saying that he would never forget when "some 7 or 8 Russian guardsmen," who had been quartered in the Grimm home for a few days while all of Europe waited for news of Napoleon's defeat, "were singing in the next room" as Wilhelm prepared the manuscript for printing.[17] Such memories of the great wars that had raged for more than a decade and through the strong years of their youth would remain with the fairy tale collaborators for the rest of their lives.

THE GOLDEN KEY

"JUST THINK, OUR FAIRY TALE LADY HAS BEEN VERY ILL AND came [to the house] recently, pale and trembling," Wilhelm wrote to Jacob about Dorothea Viehmann in December 1814, just as the very tales that Viehmann had told the brothers were being printed for volume two. "She is miserable with worry because her daughter turned up with her six children. Their father died recently. I'm going to see whether I can help a few of them into the orphanage."[1]

All their lives, Jacob and Wilhelm had known the tribulations of self-sacrificing widows and fatherless children. They had experienced that narrative plot in their own lives, and they had seen it repeated in scores of the fairy tales they had been collecting for the past eight years. The plight of Dorothea Viehmann brought them full circle, back to memories of the loss of their father, Philipp, the suffering of their mother, Dorothea, and the undying devotion of their aunts, Juliane Schlemmer and Henriette Zimmer. The brothers' own childhood had been short-lived, and somehow, the fairy tales and the remarkable women who had helped collect them had exerted a kind of redemptive power. On April 15, 1815, the brothers' beloved Aunt Zimmer died, leaving them with no more elders in the family to turn to. Dorothea Viehmann followed her that autumn on November 17, her hour of death arriving "in the evening," Wilhelm noted in the brothers' working copy of the fairy tale anthology.[2]

As this older generation of storytellers and lifelong material support to the brothers' scholarship disappeared, Jacob and Wilhelm found that the books and articles they had managed to publish during the Napoleonic era had now established a name for them in Europe. Jacob was thirty years old, Wilhelm twentynine. Together, they had laid the foundation for the decades of research that would follow in philology, medieval literature, and folklore. They wrote scores of books and articles together and independently; these, like the fairy tales, became cornerstones in the history of German literature and literary studies. The *Songs of the Old Edda, German Legends* (volumes one and two, to which the von Haxthausen and von Droste-Hülshoff sisters contributed substantially), a multivolume *German Grammar,* a *History of the German Language,* and the very ambitious *German Dictionary* are some of their most important titles. In time, the brothers received honorary doctorates from the universities of Marburg and

Berlin. They taught, for seven years, as professors at the university of Göttingen, where, in 1837, the arch-conservative sovereign, Ernst August, declared null and void the legal Constitution of that region. The brothers Grimm protested, along with several of their university colleagues, which led not only to the loss of their teaching posts but also to banishment. Their actions prompted a student revolt that hailed Jacob and Wilhelm as political heroes across most of Europe. As older men, the brothers lived in Berlin, where they worked on the voluminous *German Dictionary*, reaching as far as the word *Frucht* (fruit), before their deaths; Wilhelm passing in 1859, followed by Jacob in 1863.

❧

All the young women who had been so vital to the fairy tale publications also moved on in their adult lives. Most became mothers and wives. Some became writers of great renown. After the death of her husband, Achim, in 1831, Bettina von Arnim, having raised her seven children, began publishing her own writing at the age of fifty. She wrote two romantic epistolary works in which she situated herself in imagined or adapted relationships with other literary figures of the present and past. *Goethe's Correspondence with a Child*, published in 1835, made her famous in Germany overnight, and *Günderode: A Correspondence*, published five years later, is now considered to be a key work in the history of German women's literature.

Annette von Droste-Hülshoff also achieved fame as a writer, not publishing until her forties. Her work encompassed several genres, including an epic in verse called *The Doctor's Bequest*, two volumes of poetry, *Poems* and *The Spiritual Year*, and a novella, *The Birch of the Jew*, a mystery tale about the murder of a Jewish man, a book that made her one of Germany's leading female authors of the nineteenth century. Annette would never forget her battles with Wilhelm Grimm. Twenty-five years after her folkloric collaboration with the brothers, she wrote to a friend and told how "for years" Wilhelm had offered her only "the bitterest mockery and every kind of neglect" to the point that she "wished for [her] own death a thousand times." But then, Annette confessed, they had been very young at the time, and she had been herself "very stubborn and unhappy" because, as a young intellect of the feminine sex, she had to do whatever she could "to fight [her] way through."[3]

Marie Hassenpflug married Captain Philipp Ludwig von Dalwigk zu Schauenburg in Hoof in 1814. Six years later, at the age of thirty-two, she became court lady to the Duchess Friederike von Anhalt Bernburg. Like Dorothea Viehmann, Marie Hassenpflug did not escape the misfortune of a false identity constructed by male scholars. For more than a hundred years after the publication of volumes one and two of the *Children's and Household Fairy Tales*, Grimm researchers were led to believe that she was "old Marie," the maidservant of the Wild family, and not the highly cultivated, self-possessed lady of the court that Marie Hassenpflug became. The problem began not with Jacob and Wilhelm, but with Wilhelm's son, Herman Grimm, a German scholar who misread his father and uncle's notes in their working copies of the fairy tales and attributed Marie's stories to the wrong storyteller, thus perpetuating the myth of the uneducated, yarn-telling old maid. It was a "capital misunderstanding" that—though not caused in this instance by Jacob and Wilhelm—still reflected literary culture's long-standing need to fulfill the Grimm ideal of the *Volk*.[4]

Marie Hassenpflug's sister, Amalia (Malchen), never married. Although many men esteemed her intelligence—she was even a political advisor to her brother Ludwig when he became a minister in the Hessian government—they found her to be too self-directed, and thus, hardly marriage material. Among women, however, Amalia would cultivate extremely devoted friendships. She became exceptionally close with Annette von Droste-Hülshoff and even moved to Meerburg on Lake Constance as an older woman to live near Annette and her sister Jenny. All three women died in Meerburg and are buried there, side by side. Though Amalia did not become as well known for her writings as Bettina von Arnim and Annette von Droste-Hülshoff, she did author one novel titled *Margarethe Verflassen*, a homage to a close woman friend's life of self-sacrifice.

Lotte Grimm played an essential role in bringing the Grimm and Hassenpflug households even closer together when, in 1822, she married Ludwig Hassenpflug. Lotte lived very well with her husband in a comfortable home, and, in 1825, gave birth to their first daughter, Agnes, who five months later died from an early childhood illness. Another baby, Friedrich, followed two years later and survived, but Lotte would lose another girl named Berta, who lived just one year. In 1831, another son was born. Lotte named him Ludwig Emil after her brother the artist. As she was expecting another child in the spring of

1833, Lotte came down with a bad case of the flu and subsequently gave birth one month prematurely to a daughter, Dorothea. Though the baby survived the birth, Lotte became extremely ill. Dortchen Wild came to her side, until she, too, became so sick that she could no longer care for her dear friend. Wilhelm then stepped in, tending to Lotte until she died on June 15, 1833. She was forty years old. Amalia Hassenpflug raised Lotte's young children, bonding especially with Lotte's daughter, until Ludwig Hassenpflug remarried.

Wilhelm Grimm remained intimate friends with Jenny von Droste-Hülshoff for decades after the publications of the fairy tales. In fact, their correspondence contained the most romantic and sentimental letters Wilhelm Grimm ever wrote. It's likely that he lived in consternation for some time over whom to marry: the girl next door, Dortchen Wild, or his literary soul mate, Jenny von Droste-Hülshoff. He chose Dortchen, a woman from his own social class who took pride in her sacrifice for family, a value that also ranked highly in the Grimm home.

Wilhelm and Dortchen married in 1825. Just days after the wedding, he wrote about his wife to a fellow scholar and mentioned that he had known her since childhood: "We all have always perceived her as belonging to us. I don't believe that I, as people say, am on my honeymoon, but I have the premonition that I am going to be happy for the rest of my life, just as I have been in the past eight days. She is soulful, natural, understanding, and bright. She takes joy in the world and is nonetheless prepared in every moment to give herself over to something higher and better."[5] Like Lotte Grimm, Wilhelm and Dortchen would experience the same sad fate of losing their firstborn child, named after Jacob and lovingly called Jacöbchen, in 1826. Together, they raised three surviving children, two sons, Herman and Rudolf, and a daughter named Auguste.

Jacob was deeply attached to Dortchen Wild, too. Though he never vied for her romantic attentions the way Ferdinand had, he set up home with Dortchen and Wilhelm, and the three lived together for the rest of their lives. Dortchen often joked about her "two husbands" and assisted the brothers in the fairy tale collection through every volume and edition that was ever published. She outlived both men. On their deathbeds, she played the nurturer she had always been, so practiced had she become at being the exemplar daughter and wife, the favorite of Frau Holle.

Clemens Brentano, Jacob and Wilhelm's wayward friend, published several books of notoriety that spanned the genres of lyric poetry, essay, and romance. From 1819 to 1824, Brentano recorded the visions of the stigmatized nun Anna Katharine Emmerick, never leaving her bedside in obsessive devotion. After the nun's death, Brentano's life became exceedingly shiftless as he moved from city to city until he died in 1842. Four years later, a volume titled *The Fairy Tales* was published. Wildly different from the soberly footnoted and "faithfully" collected stories of the *Children's and Household Fairy Tales*, the volume was a loose anthology of writings, including Brentano's original poetry, stories based on legends he had collected from the region of the Rhineland, and free adaptations of Giambattista Basile's *Pentamerone*. The book was not successful by any comparison to the Grimm anthology.

After the publication of volume two of the *Children's and Household Fairy Tales*, women's participation in the project had slowed to a trickle. The von Haxthausen sisters added more stories to the repertoire, providing the brothers with ten fascinating religious fairy tales bearing titles such as "The Blessed Virgin's Little Glass," "Poverty and Humility Lead to Heaven," "Saint Joseph in the Forest," and "The Heavenly Wedding." But the soulful years of collecting stories directly from oral sources had become a thing of the past. The majority of contributors were now male, and the tales they submitted were usually texts culled from old manuscripts dug up in libraries. The familiar, "faithful" process of transcribing words as the storytellers told them aloud became the exception rather than the rule, and plans for a third volume of the anthology, especially after Dorothea Viehmann's death, were eventually abandoned.

A second edition of the *Children's and Household Fairy Tales* that included the stories from volumes one and two, some new additions, and some stories that integrated several versions of the same tale was published in 1819. Then, three years later, the brothers put out a third edition, accompanied by a separate volume of voluminous research notes. In 1823, the Grimms' fairy tales were translated into English for the first time. The book paved the way for the 1825 German edition known as the *Kleine Ausgabe* (Small Edition), which was modeled on typical fairy tale collections published in England at the time and featured fifty selected stories with exquisite illustrations executed by Ludwig Grimm. For the first time, and as Wilhelm had made the editorial changes needed to fit the moral and pedagogical expectations of the early nineteenth century, the Grimm anthology was specifically aimed at a young audience. For example, Rapunzel was no longer a pregnant maid out of wedlock, and stories such as "How Two Children Played at Slaughtering"—a gory lesson in why children shouldn't play with knives—were omitted. The *Small Edition* of the *Children's and Household Fairy Tales* marked the beginning of the Grimm legend. Selling for one round *Thaler,* it was a marketing success that won wide public approval. Fifteen hundred copies were printed, and all of them sold. By the late 1850s, before Wilhelm's death, the edition had been reprinted nine more times. The *Große Ausgabe* (Great Edition) of the fairy tales, published in 1837, was even more successful, for by that time, reading fairy stories had become all the fashion throughout Europe.

The Grimm stories have since traveled to all corners of the earth. They have been translated into more than 140 languages. In recent decades, they've rippled through popular culture as the basis of feature film productions, such as Disney's *Snow White, Sleeping Beauty,* and *Cinderella,* or DreamWorks SKG's *Shrek.* Bruno Bettelheim's *The Uses of Enchantment* made them the core material for explorations of the subconscious in Freudian psychology. Stephen Sondheim's Broadway hit, *Into the Woods,* brought the tales to the musical stage; and Angela Carter (*The Bloody Chamber*), Anne Sexton (*Transformations*), and Susanna Moore (*In the Cut,* later adapted into a film by Jane Campion) have pressed them into dark feminist retellings.

Today, many parents and educators find the Grimm fairy tales too violent for young readers, but this has always been so. The earliest critics of the *Children's and Household Fairy Tales* complained that the collection wasn't child friendly, and that the simplistic diction was much too low-brow. In a letter to his former professor, Friedrich Carl von Savigny, on December 12, 1814, Wilhelm defended the anthology: "One day it could prove that precisely that which is despised might actually be meaningful and significant."[6] As for the female collaborators, the earliest versions of the stories, as they appear in volumes one and two of the *Children's and Household Fairy Tales,* are indeed meaningful and significant, for they are the closest we will ever come to the historical women themselves. The filters of revision, retelling, and reinterpretation were at their minimum in the earliest editions, and they offer us the most direct knowledge of the tales as they existed for women of the age.

In their defense of the tales, the brothers Grimm also compared the stories they had collected to the Bible, saying that the good Book, which took pride of place in so many homes across Europe as a means of teaching children right from wrong, also possessed "questionable elements" and in far larger measure than the fairy tales themselves. "Its right usage, however, does not seek out evil," they wrote, but rather "only how a lovely word" expresses "evidence of our hearts."[7] This was a statement of tremendous foresight, for it is estimated that today the Grimms' fairy tales sell second only to the Bible in Western cultures.

❧

In May 1813, Marie Hassenpflug shared the story of "The Golden Key"[8] with the brothers Grimm. It's a very small tale that became the auspicious culminating story of the entire collection in every edition the brothers ever published. Its essence expresses the very regenerative power of the oral tradition that caused the Grimms to become so fascinated with old stories and to turn to women who could bring this mystery of transmission to light.

"One winter when there was a deep snow," the story opens, "a poor boy had to go out to fetch wood on a sled." After gathering and loading up the wood, he feels cold, so he decides to build a fire in the woods before heading home. The boy begins to sweep the snow away in the area where he wishes to build the fire, and as he reaches the bare earth, he discovers a golden key. "Now," he thinks to himself, "where there's a key, there's certainly a lock, too." Digging still further, he finds a small iron box. "Ay!" he thinks, "if only the key will fit! Surely there will be wondrous and precious things inside." He searches and searches the box, but there is no keyhole to be found, until finally, he spies a very tiny hole, and naturally, the key fits perfectly inside. He turns the key once, "and now we must wait," we're told, until the boy has turned the key completely in the lock. Then, we'll get to see just what it is that's inside.

ACKNOWLEDGMENTS

I'm grateful to my true love, Gerard, for standing by me from beginning to end as I made my way through the deep forest of this book. I thank my son, Elijah Wapner, for his humor and comradeship, particularly when I began to find my way back out of the dark woods I had sojourned in for so long. I'm forever thankful to my mother, Corrine, who traveled across the country twice to spend time with my son while I visited places in Germany where the brothers Grimm and their female collaborators lived and collected stories. I also want to say thanks to Greg and Avis for their constant warmth and openness of spirit, home, and heart.

To the Schneider family—Herbert, Hilde, Gabi, Jörg, and Stephan—I must thank you all, after twenty-four years of friendship, for introducing me to your culture, your language, and your loving home. What a joy it is for me to give back, in some small way, the enormous gift you have given me!

I thank good friends and colleagues who understand the writing life and the stubborn perseverance it demands of us: Colette Dowling, Lisa Phillips, and Gail Bradney. I'm grateful and honored to be a friend of Judy Upjohn, who, over the three years of the research and writing of this book, was a steadfast support and witness to my life unfolding. I thank Lowell Miller for his help when I was in a pinch, and the friends who helped me through the tough days: Joe Bongiorno for the after-hours typing, Greg Lofaro for his fun assistance, Taima Smith for all the places she jumped in to the rescue, and Shaina Kapeluck for her research support.

I honor and admire the archivists, folklorists, and Grimm scholars who have devoted their lives to the study of the fairy tales and their sources: Jack Zipes, Heinz Rölleke, Maria Tartar, and Marina Warner. Among these kind folks, I'm particularly grateful to Berthold Friemel, founder of the Grimm Society of Berlin, as well as his colleague Maria Hartz, who were always so welcoming and warmhearted during my visits there. I'm also grateful to Ingrid Pergande-Kaufmann for our insightful discussion about the female collaborators of the Grimm fairy tales over coffee in her cozy apartment. In Kassel, Bernhard Lauer, director of the Brothers Grimm Museum, and his helpful assistant, Frau Roggensack, helped to make my work there efficient and comfortable. I also express my deep thanks to Günter Tiggesbäumker, director of the Museum Bökerhof, who opened the doors of Bökerhof and took me on a lovely "literary car tour" through the green hilly regions where the von Haxthausens and von Droste-Hülshoffs spent their summers.

I wish to express my gratitude to the German Academic Exchange Service for a research fellowship that allowed me to spend a month touring many important sites in Hesse and Berlin and to conduct research in archives and libraries. I'm also grateful to the following programs, libraries, and institutions: Arbeitsstelle Grimm-Briefwechsel, Staatsbibliothek zu Berlin-Preußischer Kulturbesitz, the Landesbibliothek in Kassel, the Staatsarchiv Marburg, and the Humboldt-Universitätsbibliothek zu Berlin.

Finally, I wish to thank my agent, Elizabeth Kaplan, my copy editor, Jennifer Blakebrough-Raeburn, and my editors at Perseus: Amanda Cook, for her understanding of how to build this book around the female storytellers, and Megan Hustad, for her attention and devotion to narrative.

*The original library of the Brothers Grimm needs your help! If you'd like to adopt a book for refurbishing and preservation, visit www.valerieparadiz.com for directions in English.

NOTES

Prologue

1. Jacob Grimm and Wilhelm Grimm, *Kinder- und Hausmärchen. Nach der Großen Ausgabe von 1857, textkritisch revidiert, kommentiert und durch Register erschlossen,* ed. Hans-Jörg Uther, 7th ed. (Darmstadt: Wissenschaftliche Buchgesellschaft, 1996), "The Frog Prince," no. 1.

2. Jacob Grimm and Wilhelm Grimm, *Kinder- und Hausmärchen gesammelt durch die Brüder Grimm,* enlarged reprint of the two-volume first edition of 1812 and 1815, according to the working copy of Brother Grimm Museum of Kassel with handwritten corrections and notes by the brothers Grimm, ed. Heinz Rölleke and Ulrike Marquardt (Göttingen: Vandenhoeck & Ruprecht, 1986), 1:xiv.

3. Marina Warner, *From the Beast to the Blonde: On Fairy Tales and Their Tellers* (New York: Farrar, Straus and Giroux, 1994), 17.

4. Ibid.

5. Ibid., 18.

Chapter 1

1. Jacob Grimm in Dieter Hennig and Bernhard Lauer, eds., *200 Jahre Brüder Grimm: Dokumente ihres Lebens und Wirkens* (Kassel: Verlag Weber & Weidenmeyer, 1985), 143.

2. Ibid.

3. Ibid.

4. Uther, *Kinder- und Hausmärchen,* "The Devil with Three Golden Hairs," no. 29.

5. Hennig and Lauer, *200 Jahre Brüder Grimm*, 142.

6. Ibid., 157.

7. Ibid.

8. Henriette Zimmer to Dorothea Zimmer, Kassel, September 4, 1798, SBPK, Berlin, Brüder Grimm Nachlaß, NG 407, reprinted in Hennig and Lauer, *200 Jahre Brüder Grimm*, 169.

9. Wilhelm Schoof, *Wilhelm Grimm: Aus seinem Leben* (Bonn: Dümmler Verlag, 1960), 18.

10. Dorothea Grimm to Wilhelm Grimm, October 27, 1798, in Schoof, *Wilhelm Grimm*, 24.

11. Hermann Zimmer to Jacob Grimm and Wilhelm Grimm, October 6, 1798, in Schoof, *Wilhelm Grimm*, 56.

12. Wilhelm Grimm, 19.

13. Wilhelm Grimm to Dorothea Grimm, Kassel, September 30, 1798, HAS Marburg: Gr. 340 Br. 2657.13. Wilhelm Grimm, 19.

14. Dorothea Grimm to Jacob Grimm, November 19, 1798, in Wilhelm Schoof, *Jacob Grimm: Aus Seinem Leben* (Bonn: Dümmler Verlag, 1960), 66.

15. Ibid.

16. Uther, *Kinder- und Hausmärchen*, "Rumplstiltskin," no. 55.

17. Dorothea Grimm to Jacob Grimm, November 19, 1798, in Wilhelm Schoof, *Jacob Grimm: Aus Seinem Leben* (Bonn: Dümmler Verlag, 1960), 66.

18. Dorothea Grimm to Jacob Grimm and Wilhelm Grimm, November 22, 1798, in Schoof, *Jacob Grimm*, 67–68.

19. Uther, *Kinder- und Hausmärchen*, "The Wolf and the Seven Goat Kids," no. 5.

Chapter 2

1. Schoof, *Jacob Grimm: Aus seinem Leben*, 78.

2. Ibid.

3. Schoof, *Wilhelm Grimm: Aus seinem Leben*, 103.

4. Ibid.

5. Schoof, *Jacob Grimm: Aus seinem Leben*, 87.

6. Ibid., 83.

7. Jacob Grimm to Henriette Zimmer, January 20, 1805, HAS Marburg: 340 Grimm Br. 2272, reprinted in Hennig and Lauer *200 Jahre Brüder Grimm*, 180.

8. Jacob Grimm to Dorothea Grimm, January 20, 1805, SBPK Berlin: Nachlaß Grimm 383, reprinted in Hennig and Lauer *200 Jahre Brüder Grimm*, 180–181.

9. Jacob Grimm to Henriette Zimmer, January 23, 1805, HSA Marburg: 340 Grimm Br. 2273, reprinted in Hennig and Lauer, *200 Jahre Brüder Grimm*, 181.

10. Wilhelm Grimm to Jacob Grimm, February 2–13, 1805, no. 7, Jacob Grimm and Wilhelm Grimm, *Briefwechsel zwischen Jacob und Wilhelm Grimm*, ed. Heinz Rölleke, vol. 1 (Stuttgart: S. Hirzel Verlag, 2001).

11. Jacob Grimm to Wilhelm Grimm, February 10, 1805, no. 6, in Rölleke, *Briefwechsel*.

12. Ibid., March 1 and 6, 1805, no. 10.

13. Ibid., July 12, 1805, no. 30.

14. Ibid., August 4, 1805, no. 31.

15. Jacob Grimm to Henriette Zimmer and Dorothea Grimm, September 7, 1805, SBPK Berlin: Nachlaß Grimm, 410.

16. H. A. Frenzel and E. Frenzel, *Daten deutscher Dichtung: Chronologischer Abriß der deutschen Literaturgeschichte*, Bd. 2 (Munich: dtv, 1986), 320.

17. Clemens Brentano to Achim von Arnim, October 19, 1807, in Wilhelm Schoof, *Zur Entstehungsgeschichte der Grimmschen Märchen* (Hamburg: Dr. Ernst Hauswedell & Co, 1959), 11.

Chapter 3

1. Uther, *Kinder- und Hausmärchen*, "Child of Mary," no. 3.

2. These pages are a synopsis of the anecdotes that Auguste Grimm wrote about Dorothea's memories of her own childhood. They appear in "Erinnerungen Dortchen Grimms in der Aufzeichnung ihrer Tochter Auguste," *Brüder Grimm Gedenken*, vol. 15, ed. Berthold Friemel (Stuttgart: S. Hirzel Verlag, 2003), 1–15.

3. Uther, *Kinder- und Hausmärchen*, "The Wedding of Mrs. Fox," no. 38.

4. Uther, *Kinder- und Hausmärchen*, 4:78–79.

5. Ibid.

6. Warner, *From the Beast to the Blonde: On Fairy Tales and Their Tellers*, xxv.

Chapter 4

1. Jacob Grimm to Henriette Zimmer, May 27, 1808, in Schoof, *Wilhelm Grimm: Aus seinem Leben*, 67–68.

2. Ibid., 68.

3. Schoof, *Jacob Grimm: Aus seinem Leben*, 117.

4. Ibid., 140.

5. Ibid., 140–141.

6. Ibid., 118.

7. Ibid., 174.

8. Wilhelm Schoof, "Zur Entstehungsgeschichte der Grimm'schen Märchen," *Hessische Blätter für Volkskunde* 29 (1930): 46.

9. Wilhelm Grimm to Jacob Grimm, September 10, 1808, no. 40, in Rölleke, *Briefwechsel*.

10. Ibid.

11. Ibid.

12. Jacob Grimm to Achim von Arnim, May 20, 1811, trans. Jack Zipes, in *The Brothers Grimm: From Enchanted Forests to the Modern World*, 2nd ed. (New York: Palgrave/Macmillan, 2002), 11.

13. Rölleke und Marquardt *Kinder- und Hausmärchen gesammelt durch die Brüder Grimm*, "Fitcher's Bird," no. 46.

14. Ibid., no. 52.

15. Schoof, "Zur Entstehungsgeschichte der Grimm'schen Märchen," 50.

16. Ibid., 51.

17. Ibid., 52.

18. Ibid., 54.

19. Ibid., 53.

20. Ibid., 51.

21. Ibid., 55.

22. Ibid., 54.

23. Ibid., 56.

24. Ibid.

Chapter 5

1. Achim von Arnim to Clemens Brentano, December 8, 1808, in Wilhelm Praesent, ed., *Ludwig Emil Grimm: Erinnerungen aus meinem Leben* (Kassel and Basel: Bärenreiter Verlag, 1950), 547.

2. Henriette Zimmer to Lotte Grimm, June 20, 1808, in *Briefe an Lotte Grimm,* ed. Else Hünert-Hofmann (Kassel and Basel: Bärenreiter Verlag, 1972), 41–42.

3. Wilhelm Grimm to Jacob Grimm, April 1, 1809, no. 41, in Rölleke, *Briefwechsel.*

4. Ibid.

5. Ibid., April 10, 1809, no. 42.

6. Ibid.

7. Ibid.

8. Jacob Grimm to Wilhelm Grimm, April 15, 1809, no. 44, in Rölleke, *Briefwechsel.*

9. Wilhelm Grimm to Jacob Grimm, April 21 and 22, 1809, no. 45, in Rölleke, *Briefwechsel.*

10. Ibid., May 24–28, 1809, no. 52.

11. Ibid., c. June 15, 1809, no. 60.

12. Ibid., June 18, 1809, no. 56.

13. Ibid., April 21 and 22, 1809, no. 45.

14. Rölleke and Marquardt, *Kinder- und Hausmärchen gesammelt durch die Brüder Grimm,* "The Six Swans," no. 49.

15. Jacob Grimm to Wilhelm Grimm, May 17, 1809, no. 51, in Rölleke, *Briefwechsel.*

16. Wilhelm Grimm to Jacob Grimm, September 15–18, 1809, no. 73, in Rölleke, *Briefwechsel.*

17. Ferdinand Grimm to Lotte Grimm, August 18, 1809, in Hünert-Hofmann, *Briefe an Lotte Grimm,* 80–81.

18. Wilhelm Grimm to Jacob Grimm, August 13, 1809, in Hünert-Hofmann, *Briefe an Lotte Grimm,* no. 67.

19. Jacob Grimm to Wilhelm Grimm, August 16, 1809, in Hünert-Hofmann, *Briefe an Lotte Grimm,* no. 68.

20. Ibid., September 10, 1809, no. 72.

21. Wilhelm Grimm to Jacob Grimm, September 15–18, 1809, in Hünert-Hofmann, *Briefe an Lotte Grimm,* no. 73.

22. Ibid.

23. Ibid.

24. Jacob Grimm to Wilhelm Grimm, November 11, 1809, in Hünert-Hofmann, *Briefe an Lotte Grimm,* no. 79.

Chapter 6

1. Jacob Grimm to Wilhelm Grimm, September 3, 1809, no. 71, in Rölleke, *Briefwechsel.*

2. Rölleke and Marquardt, *Kinder- und Hausmärchen gesammelt durch die Brüder Grimm,* no. 14.

3. Ibid., "The Maiden with No Hands," no. 31.

4. Uther, *Kinder- und Hausmärchen,* 4:68–69.

5. Rölleke and Marquardt, *Kinder- und Hausmärchen gesammelt durch die Brüder Grimm*, 138.

6. Heinz Rölleke, *Die Märchen der Brüder Grimm: Eine Einführung* (Bonn, Berlin: Bouvier Verlag, 1972), 78.

7. Rölleke and Marquardt, *Kinder- und Hausmärchen gesammelt durch die Brüder Grimm*, "Bluebeard," no. 62.

Chapter 7

1. Dortchen Wild to Lotte Grimm, autumn 1808, in Hünert-Hofmann, *Briefe an Lotte Grimm*, 127.

2. Ibid.

3. Ibid.

4. Schoof, *Wilhelm Grimm: Aus seinem Leben*, 196.

5. Jacob Grimm to Achim von Arnim, in Adolf Stoll, *Ludwig Grimm: Erinnerungen aus meinem Leben* (Leipzig: Hesse & Becker, 1913), 547.

6. Jacob Grimm to Achim von Arnim, March 22, 1811, in Helmut Henne and Birgit Richter, eds., *Der unbekannte Grimm: Ferdinand und seine Brüder* (Braunschweig: Johann Heinrich Meyer Verlag, 1988), 9–10.

7. Jacob Grimm to Wilhelm Grimm, October 18, 1809, no. 77, in Rölleke, *Briefwechsel*.

8. Ferdinand Grimm to Lotte Grimm, August 18, 1809, in Hünert-Hofmann, *Briefe an Lotte Grimm*, 80–81.

9. Wilhelm Grimm in Hans Daffis, *Inventar der Grimm-Schränke in der Preussischen Staatsbibliothek* (Leipzig: Verlag von Karl W. Hiersemann, 1923), 112–113.

10. Rölleke and Marquardt, *Kinder- und Hausmärchen gesammelt durch die Brüder Grimm*, "The Singing Bone," no. 28.

11. Stoll, *Ludwig Grimm*, 214.

12. Ibid., 551.

13. Frank McLynn, *Napoleon: A Biography* (New York: Arcade, 1997), 445.

14. Rölleke and Marquardt, *Kinder- und Hausmärchen gesammelt durch die Brüder Grimm*, "Frau Holle," no. 24.

Chapter 8

1. Schoof, *Zur Entstehungsgeschichte der Grimmschen Märchen*, 34.

2. Ibid.

3. Ibid.

4. Ibid., 34–35.

5. Rölleke and Marquardt, *Kinder- und Hausmärchen gesammelt durch die Brüder Grimm*, "Red Riding Hood," no. 26.

6. Schoof, *Zur Entstehungsgeschichte der Grimmschen Märchen*, 35.

7. Ibid., 35–36.

8. Ibid., "The Magic Table, the Golden Donkey, and the Club in the Sack," no. 36.

9. McLynn, *Napoleon*, 526.

10. Schoof, *Wilhelm Grimm: Aus seinem Leben*, 211.

11. Rölleke and Marquardt, *Kinder- und Hausmärchen gesammelt durch die Brüder Grimm*, v–vi.

Chapter 9

1. Wilhelm Grimm to Jacob Grimm, August 19, 1811, in Schoof, *Zur Entstehungsgeschichte der Grimmschen Märchen*, 49.

2. Ibid.

3. Wilhelm Grimm to Ludowine von Haxthausen, January 21, 1813, Kassel, in Alexander Reisserscheid, ed., *Freundesbriefe von Wilhelm und Jacob Grimm* (Heilbronn, Verlag von Gebr. Henninger, 1878), 1–2.

4. Ibid., 4.

5. Rölleke and Marquardt, *Kinder- und Hausmärchen gesammelt durch die Brüder Grimm,* "The Maiden of Brakel," no. 53.

6. Jack Zipes, ed. and trans., *The Complete Tales of the Brothers Grimm* (New York: Bantam, 1992), 490.

7. Ludowine von Haxthausen to Wilhelm Grimm, undated, in Schoof, *Zur Entstehungsgeschichte der Grimmschen Märchen,* 98.

8. Rölleke and Marquardt, *Kinder- und Hausmärchen gesammelt durch die Brüder Grimm,* "Devil Greencoat," no. 15.

9. McLynn, *Napoleon,* 547.

10. Reisserscheid, *Freundesbriefe von Wilhelm und Jacob Grimm,* 16.

11. Hennig and Lauer, *200 Jahre Brüder Grimm,* 550.

12. Ibid.

13. K. Schulte-Kemminghausen, ed., *Briefwechsel zwischen Wilhelm Grimm und Jenny von Droste-Hülshoff* (Münster: Aschendorffsche Verlagsbuchhandlung, 1929), 10.

14. Hennig and Lauer, *200 Jahre Brüder Grimm,* 550.

15. Rölleke and Marquardt, *Kinder- und Hausmärchen gesammelt durch die Brüder Grimm,* "The Worn Out Dancing Shoes," no. 47.

16. Schulte-Kemminghausen, *Briefwechsel zwischen Wilhelm Grimm und Jenny von Droste-Hülshoff,* 13–14.

Chapter 10

1. Wilhelm Grimm to Ferdinand Grimm, in Hennig and Lauer, *200 Jahre Brüder Grimm,* 545.

2. Schoof, *Jacob Grimm: Aus seinem Leben,* 139–140.

3. Rölleke and Marquardt, *Kinder- und Hausmärchen gesammelt durch die Brüder Grimm,* 2:iv.

4. Uther, *Kinder- und Hausmärchen,* 4:46–48.

5. Rölleke and Marquardt, *Kinder- und Hausmärchen gesammelt durch die Brüder Grimm,* 2:v.

6. Ibid., "The Goose Maid," no. 3, vol. 2.

7. Uther, *Kinder- und Hausmärchen*, 4:170.

8. Rölleke and Marquardt, *Kinder- und Hausmärchen gesammelt durch die Brüder Grimm*, "Doctor Know It All," no. 12, vol. 2.

9. Ibid., 2: iii–xii.

Chapter 11

1. Diary entry of Ludwig Grimm's future wife, in Rölleke, *Briefwechsel.*

2. Jacob Grimm to Achim von Arnim, November 17, 1813, in Schoof, *Jacob Grimm: Aus seinem Leben*, 118–119.

3. Ibid.

4. Jacob Grimm to Wilhelm Grimm, January 20, 1814, no. 127, in Rölleke, *Briefwechsel.*

5. Ibid.

6. Wilhelm Grimm to Jacob Grimm, January 18 and 24, 1814, no. 129.

7. Ibid.

8. Wilhelm Grimm to Jacob Grimm, February 9, 1814, no. 132.

9. Wilhelm Grimm to Jacob Grimm, March 8 and 9, 1814, no. 136.

10. Ibid.

11. Jacob Grimm to Wilhelm Grimm, March 19, 1814, no. 138.

12. Rölleke and Marquardt, *Kinder- und Hausmärchen gesammelt durch die Brüder Grimm*, vol. 2, "The Three Army Surgeons," no. 32.

13. Jacob Grimm to Wilhelm Grimm, April 19–25, 1814, no. 145 in Rölleke, *Briefwechsel* .

14. Schulte-Kemminghausen, *Briefwechsel zwischen Wilhelm Grimm und Jenny von Droste-Hülshoff*, 22–23.

15. Reisserscheid, *Freundesbriefe von Wilhelm und Jacob Grimm*, 25.

16. Ibid.

17. Schulte-Kemminghausen, *Briefwechsel zwischen Wilhelm Grimm und Jenny von Droste-Hülshoff*, 25.

Chapter 12

1. Schoof, *Zur Entstehungsgeschichte der Grimmschen Märchen*, 64.

2. Hennig and Lauer, *200 Jahre Brüder Grimm*, 546.

3. Schulte-Kemminghausen, *Briefwechsel zwischen Wilhelm Grimm und Jenny von Droste-Hülshoff*, 11.

4. Heinz Rölleke, "Die 'stockhessischen' Märchen der 'Alten Marie,'" in *Die Märchen der Brüder Grimm: Quellen und Studien* (Trier: Wissenschaftlicher Buchverlag, 2000), 9.

5. Schoof, *Wilhelm Grimm: Aus seinem Leben*, 199.

6. Rölleke, *Die Märchen der Brüder Grimm*, 78.

7. Rölleke and Marquardt, *Kinder- und Hausmärchen gesammelt durch die Brüder Grimm*, 2:viii–x.

8. Ibid., vol. 2, no. 70.

BIBLIOGRAPHY

Fairy Tale Editions

Grimm, Jacob, and Wilhelm Grimm. *Kinder- und Hausmärchen. Nach der Großen Ausgabe von 1857, textkritisch revidiert, kommentiert und durch Register erschlossen.* Edited by Hans-Jörg Uther. 7th ed. Darmstadt: Wissenschaftliche Buchgesellschaft, 1996.

_____. *Kinder- und Hausmärchen gesammelt durch die Brüder Grimm.* Enlarged reprint of the two-volume first edition of 1812 and 1815, according to the working copy of the Brother Grimms Museum of Kassel, with handwritten corrections and notes by the brothers Grimm. Edited by Heinz Rölleke and Ulrike Marquardt. 2 vols. Göttingen: Vandenhoeck & Ruprecht, 1986.

Rölleke, Heinz, ed. *Grimms Märchen: Ausgewählt und mit einem Kommentar versehen.* Frankfurt: Suhrkamp, 1998.

Zipes, Jack, ed. and trans. *The Complete Tales of the Brothers Grimm.* New York: Bantam, 1992.

Correspondence and Other Primary Sources

Friemel, Berthold, ed. "Erinnerungen Dortchen Grimms in der Aufzeichnung ihrer Tochter Auguste," *Brüder Grimm Gedenken.* Vol. 15. Stuttgart: S. Hirzel Verlag, 2003.

Hünert-Hofmann, Else, ed. *Briefe an Lotte Grimm.* Kassel and Basel: Bärenreiter Verlag, 1972.

Reisserscheid, Alexander, ed. *Freundesbriefe von Wilhelm und Jacob Grimm.* Heilbronn: Verlag von Gebr. Henninger, 1878.

Rölleke, Heinz, ed. *Briefwechsel zwischen Jacob und Wilhelm Grimm.* Vol. 1. Stuttgart: S. Hirzel Verlag, 2001.

Schulte-Kemminghausen, K., ed. *Briefwechsel zwischen Wilhelm Grimm und Jenny von Droste-Hülshoff.* Münster: Aschendorffsche Verlagsbuchhandlung, 1929.

Reference Works

Bolte, Johannes, and Georg Polivka. *Anmerkungen zu den "Kinder- und Hausmärchen."* 5 vols., 1913–1932. Hildesheim: Georg Olms, 1963.

Daffis, Hans. *Inventar der Grimm-Schränke in der Preußischen Staatsbibliothek.* Leipzig: Verlag von Karl W. Hiersemann, 1923.

Denecke, Ludwig. *Jacob Grimm und sein Bruder Wilhelm.* Stuttgart: Metzler, 1971.

Frenzel, H. A., and E. Frenzel. *Daten deutscher Dichtung: Chronologischer Abriß der deutschen Literaturgeschichte.* Bd. 2. Munich: dtv, 1986.

Gates, David. *The Napoleonic Wars 1803-1815.* London and New York: Arnold, 1997.

Gestner, Hermann. *Brüder Grimm in Selbstzeugnissen und Bilddokumenten.* Reinbek bei Hamburg: Rowohlt, 1973.

Henne, Helmut, and Birgit Richter, eds. *Der unbekannte Grimm: Ferdinand und seine Brüder.* Braunschweig: Johann Heinrich Meyer Verlag, 1988.

Hennig, Dieter, and Bernhard Lauer, eds. *200 Jahre Brüder Grimm: Dokumente ihres Lebens und Wirkens.* 3 vols. Kassel: Verlag Weber & Weidenmeyer, 1985.

Hettinga, Donald. *The Brothers Grimm: Two Lives, One Legacy.* New York: Clarion, 2001.

Hildebrandt, Irma. *Es waren ihrer Fünf: Die Brüder Grimm und ihre Familie.* Köln: Diederichs, 1984.

Hoffmann, Gerd, and Heinz Rölleke. *Der unbekannte Bruder Grimm.* Düsseldorf: Diederichs, 1979.

Losch, Philipp. "Male: Eine Virtuosin der Freundschaft." Grimm Sammlung, Typoskript 1. Grimm-Museum, Kassel.

————. "Male Hassenpflug." *Zietschrift des Vereins für hessische Geschichte und Landeskunde* 53 (1952): 104–111.

McLynn, Frank. *Napoleon: A Biography.* New York: Arcade, 1997.

Murphy, J. Ronald. *The Owl, the Raven and the Dove: The Religious Meaning of the Grimms' Magic Fairy Tales.* Oxford: Oxford University Press, 2000.

Ohles, Fredreick. *Germany's Rude Awakening: Censorship in the Land of the Brothers Grimm.* Kent, Ohio: Kent State University Press, 1992.

Praesent, Wilhelm, ed. *Ludwig Emil Grimm: Erinnerungen aus seinem Leben.* Kassel and Basel: Bärenreiter Verlag, 1950.

Rölleke, Heinz. *Die Märchen der Brüder Grimm: Eine Einführung.* Bonn and Berlin: Bouvier Verlag, 1972.

————. "Die 'stockhessischen' Märchen der 'Alten Marie.'" In *Die Märchen der Brüder Grimm: Quellen und Studien.* Trier: Wissenschaftlicher Buchverlag, 2000.

Schoof, Wilhelm. *Jacob Grimm: Aus seinem Leben.* Bonn: Dümmler Verlag, 1961.

————. *Wilhelm Grimm: Aus seinem Leben.* Bonn: Dümmler Verlag, 1960.

————. *Zur Entstehungsgeschichte der Grimmschen Märchen.* Hamburg: Hauswedell & Co, 1959.

————. "Zur Entstehungsgeschichte der Grimm'schen Märchen." *Hessische Blätter für Volkskunde* 29 (1930): 46.

Seitz, Gabriele. *Die Brüder Grimm: Leben-Werk-Zeit.* München: Winckler, 1984.

Stoll, Adolf. *Ludwig Grimm: Erinnerungen aus meinem Leben.* Leipzig: Hesse & Becker, 1913.

Tatar, Maria. *The Hard Facts of the Grimms' Fairy Tales.* Princeton and Oxford: Princeton University Press, 1987.

————. *Off With Their Heads! Fairy Tales and the Culture of Childhood.* Princeton: Princeton University Press, 1992.

Tiggesbäumker, Günter. *Bökerhof: Das Haus, seine Geschichte und seine Bewohner.* Brakel-Bökendorf: Bökerhof Gesellschaft e.V., 2000.

Warner, Marina. *From the Beast to the Blonde: On Fairy Tales and Their Tellers.* New York: Farrar, Straus and Giroux, 1994.

Zipes, Jack. *The Brothers Grimm: From Enchanted Forests to the Modern World.* 2d ed. New York: Palgrave/Macmillan, 2002.

INDEX